I0821711

AN ORNAMENT TO THE CITY

AN ORNAMENT TO THE CITY

Old Mobile Ironwork

John S. Sledge

Mobile Historic Development Commission

Photography by Sheila Hagler

THE UNIVERSITY OF GEORGIA PRESS

Athens and London

Designed by Robin McDonald
Set in 12/18.3 Cochin
Printed and bound by Kings Time Printing

The paper in this book meets the guidelines for permanence and durability of the Committee on Production Guidelines for Book Longevity of the Council on Library Resources.

Printed in China
10 09 08 07 06 C 5 4 3 2 1

Library of Congress Cataloging-in-Publication Data

Sledge, John S. (John Sturdivant), 1957–
An ornament to the city : old Mobile ironwork / John S. Sledge ; photography by Sheila Hagler.
p. cm.
Includes bibliographical references and index.
ISBN-13 978-0-8203-2700-6 (cloth : alk. paper) — ISBN-10 0-8203-2700-X (cloth : alk. paper)
1. Architectural ironwork—Alabama—Mobile—History. 2. Decorative cast-ironwork—Alabama—Mobile—History. I. Title.
NK8212.S55 2006
739.09761'22—dc22
2005028161

British Library Cataloging-in-Publication Data available

Published through the generosity of

THE A. S. MITCHELL FOUNDATION

Mobile, Alabama

IN MEMORY OF MY FATHER, E. B. SLEDGE

Naturalist, historian, author, sage counselor, and friend

His integrity and humor continue to inspire

Contents

Preface

Ancient Echoes (Woodrow Wilson)

OCTOBER 27, 1913, DAWNED BLUSTERY AND overcast in downtown Mobile. A strong north wind flecked with rain augured an uncomfortable day as it swirled the live oak treetops in crazy eddies, buffeted the bunting and patriotic banners that decorated Bienville Square, and whisked hats off the heads of scrambling pedestrians. Mobilians' spirits, however, were undaunted by the bitter blast. Woodrow Wilson, the twenty-eighth president of the United States, had arrived during the wee hours aboard his luxuriantly appointed Pullman car and was to spend an eventful day in their fair city.[1]

Wilson had come to Mobile to deliver a major policy address at the Fifth Annual Meeting of the Southern Commercial Congress, but his schedule also included a breakfast with local business and professional elites at the Battle House Hotel, an automobile parade along Government Street, and a public speech at Bienville Square (subsequently canceled by his personal physician because of the chill).[2]

For a brief moment the world's attention was focused on Alabama's seaport, and its residents were bursting with pride and anxious to be recognized as the "Queen City of the Gulf."[3] The *Mobile Register* that morning warmly welcomed the chief executive and displayed a two-page panoramic photograph of downtown's "modern, progressive" skyline.[4] The image depicted recently constructed multistory edifices like the Van Antwerp Building, the Bienville and Battle House Hotels, and the City Bank thrusting above the trees and dwarfing the surrounding smaller, older brick stores and warehouses. This was very much how Mobile's boosters and public men wanted their city to be perceived—as an energetic metropolis rising above its past.[5]

President Woodrow Wilson tours Mobile. Richard Vipon Taylor is seated at his left, face partially obscured by a top hat. (Courtesy Erik Overbey Collection, University of South Alabama Archives.)

The president's official local escort was Richard Vipon Taylor, vice president of the Mobile and Ohio Railroad and chairman of the Chamber of Commerce's Entertainment Committee. Taylor was an excellent choice for this responsibility—self-made, well connected, practical, pithy, and not at all starstruck.[6] In an unpublished memoir penned sometime during the 1930s, he recalled Wilson's visit as "a pleasant and important episode in my life."[7] He described the highlights of that day, beginning with his introduction of the president at the Battle House breakfast. With a delicious meal waiting, Taylor eschewed a golden opportunity to discourse and kept his remarks brief, for which Wilson good-naturedly thanked him.

After breakfast the dignitaries removed several blocks to the Lyric Theater at Joachim and Conti streets, where the president delivered his speech. When Wilson declared, to the audience's surprise, that the United States would never acquire additional territory, Taylor chuckled and whispered to a man seated beside him, "He should have added 'As far as I know.'"[8]

The presidential parade was next. Fortunately, the threat of rain had vanished and the cloud deck was breaking apart, revealing patches of powder blue sky. Excited Mobilians of all ages, bundled against the cold and grasping little American flags, lined the route and jostled one another for a better view. The thirty-five-vehicle motorcade formed opposite the stage door on Joachim Street, advanced a short block south to Government Street, and then rounded the corner and proceeded west. Taylor, clad in overcoat and top hat like the other dignitaries, was seated on Wilson's left in the presidential car.[9]

Up to this point the president's impressions of Mobile were likely fragmentary and hurried. Now, however, comfortably ensconced in his touring car with a knowledgeable guide at his elbow, he had time to enjoy the sights and learn something about the town. Government Street itself was probably the first thing he noticed. The city's principal thoroughfare, it was fully one hundred feet wide and shaded by

This elegant Italianate commercial building with its two-story verandah was photographed about the time of Wilson's visit. Located at the northwest corner of Dauphin and Royal streets, it was easily visible to the president from the Battle House. Wilson was fascinated by the Port City's decorative ironwork. (Courtesy Erik Overbey Collection, University of South Alabama Archives.)

a continuous canopy of live oak trees festooned with Spanish moss. Offices, stores, churches, and homes were handsomely situated on spacious, informally landscaped lots surrounded by elegant cast iron fences. Taylor would have pointed out the principal landmarks, many of them antebellum, and mentioned something of their history—columned masterpieces like McGill Institute, Government Street Presbyterian Church, and Barton Academy—and local civic headquarters like that of the Fidelia Club, sporting a handsome cast iron balcony. Nor would he have neglected the spectacular private residences—two- and three-story Queen Anne mansions with complex rooflines and wrap-around porches framed by gingerbread, and beautifully proportioned Federal and Italianate town houses with tall doorways and attached iron verandahs. Among the houses to which he might have directed the president's particular attention were the childhood home of Gilded Age socialite Alva Smith Vanderbilt Belmont, a Tudor Revival structure at the corner of Conception Street and, closer to Broad, the Admiral Semmes House, the in-town domicile of the late Confederate sea dog, a two-story Federal style structure with intricate iron lace.[10]

Wilson was captivated by this older, graceful Mobile and urged Taylor "never to permit, if possible, the destruction of the old time residences." He was especially charmed by the abundance of ironwork "so freely in evidence" and further enjoined his guide to preserve it as an eloquent reminder of the city's "ancient inhabitants." Taylor expressed regret in his memoir that during the intervening decades Mobilians had done just the opposite, reducing Government Street to a ghost of its former self.[11]

President Wilson's appreciative notice of Mobile's ironwork is important because it was among the earliest by an outsider. For the president, Mobile's rich display of ornamental iron—its spindly balconies, heavy lace verandahs, fancy fences and gates, fluted columns and lampposts, rococo fountains, quaint statuary, ornate benches, quirky hitching posts, and faux Venetian storefronts and facades—was character defining, setting the city apart in a far more profound way than its modern skyline touted by boosters. Sadly, it was to be decades before most Mobilians themselves shared this conviction. Consequently, much was lost to demolition, wartime scrap drives, vandalism, and neglect. Despite this lamentable attrition, however, enough survives to lend poetry and class to city cemeteries, parks, courtyards, and streets. Whether lovingly restored, or loose, rusty, and broken, Mobile's ornamental ironwork represents a priceless cultural legacy that continues to fascinate and beguile visitors and residents alike.

Acknowledgments

IN RESEARCHING AND WRITING THIS BOOK, I HAVE benefited from the kindness and resourcefulness of many fine people. To begin with, heartfelt thanks go to Joseph Meaher, Augustine Meaher III, David Dukes, Judge Brevard Hand, Frank Vincent, and Kenneth Vincent at the A. S. Mitchell Foundation for so generously underwriting publication costs. This book would not have been possible without their enduring commitment to document and celebrate Mobile's distinctive architectural history.

Three individuals in particular paved the way for this project, and I am profoundly indebted to them. They include local attorney and "arbiter elegantiae" Palmer C. Hamilton, who was an early advocate; Steve Walker, former executive director of Historic and Downtown Redevelopment for the City of Mobile; and Devereaux Bemis, director of the Historic Development Commission, who generously allowed me the office time to research and write.

Other people within city government deserve mention and praise. First, former mayor Michael C. Dow has been a steadfast and enthusiastic supporter of historic preservation for many years. His successor, Sam Jones, has now assumed this mantel. Secondly, my colleagues at the MHDC, Anne Crutcher, Ed Hooker, Kathleen Moore, and Shaun Wilson, have graciously tolerated my preoccupation with iron lace and bleary-eyed absentmindedness from too many hours in the records or at the computer. Lastly, retired urban planner Bailey du Mont greatly assisted with early files and photographs and freely shared his encyclopedic knowledge of local history.

Significant research help came from numerous institutions and people. At the University of South Alabama Archives, Michael Thomason, Elisa Baldwin, Barbara Asmus, and Erin Skaret rendered cheerful and fruitful assistance with old photographs, images, and maps. At the Historic Mobile Preservation Society, Marilyn Culpepper and Christine Cramer allowed free access to their incredibly rich collection and provided every conceivable aid. Dr. Bert Eichold and Eunice Willis at the Mobile County Health Department and Cathi Clarke at Barton Academy were also helpful, as were Coll'ette King at Mobile County Probate Court, Charlotte Chamberlain at the Local History and Genealogy branch of the Mobile Public Library, Ned Harkins and Zennia Calhoun at the Mobile Municipal Archives, and those splendid folks at the Museum of Mobile, George Ewert, Sheila Flanagan, and Charles Torrey. Tennant McWilliams at the University of Alabama in Birmingham and Arthur Scully and Ann Masson in New Orleans were of inestimable assistance.

Many others provided encouragement, help, friendship, and advice, and I humbly acknowledge their support. They include Roy Hoffman, E. C. LeVert, Nicholas Holmes III, Tom Root, Ashley Grantham, Cammie East and Bill Finch of the *Mobile Register*, Ann Howell, Franklin Daugherty, W. Barksdale Maynard, Robert Gamble of the Alabama Historical Commission, Cissy Helms, Douglas Kearley, Leo Kling, Barbara Holley Reid, Holley Margarette Reid, Elizabeth Sanders, Mary Jane "Iron" Inge, Eliska Morgan, Tommy McGehee, Rev. J. Taylor Abbot, Jay Watkins, Paula M. Watkins, the wonderful Sisters at the Visitation Monastery, Kirk Savage, Fitz Brundage, and Scott Howell at Robinson Iron in Alexander City. I am also deeply grateful for University of Georgia Press director Nicole Mitchell's involvement. Her intelligence, professionalism, and keen editorial sensibilities have made this a much better book than it otherwise would have been.

Thanks as well to the extraordinarily talented Sheila Hagler and her partner, Peggy Denniston, for the wonderful photographs in this volume. Sheila's artistic eye and Peggy's infallible judgment continue to be an inspiration. As ever, my children, Elena and Matthew, showed me unbounded and unconditional love. My beautiful wife, Lynn, provided early editorial comments that significantly improved the manuscript. Needless to say, any errors of fact herein must be charged solely to my account.

Detail, fence, Richards House.

Photographer's Note

SCIENTISTS THEORIZE THAT OUR SUN IS DYING, peeling off its outer shell a little bit every year, leaving a tiny particle of iron at its core.

Iron. When I was asked to work on a second book with John, I didn't know much about it except for the obvious: we need it (iron-poor blood makes us tired); it is in great abundance; it rusts; we cook with it; and here, in Alabama, we have the Iron Bowl. I have grown up hearing mention of the two basic types of iron but never understood their differences: cast iron vs. wrought iron. So I got out my 1953 *Encyclopedia Britannica*, volume 12, to read about it. Understanding more helped me approach the subject on a deeper level, an essential process for me. I must view the object on the ground glass in an "artistic" way, which means that my heart and intellect need to be involved.

While the magic begins on the ground glass, the darkroom is where the essence of the subject comes to life. In my tiny darkroom (a 1953 Tag-a-long converted fourteen years ago) something major happens every time I make a photograph: light-charged silver particles emerge into black-and-white tones in the developer tray before my eyes. I remain, after twenty-five years, in awe of the process.

The wonderful, mysterious sun provides the light energy necessary to bring that which is at its core, iron, to life as a beautiful, black-and-white gelatin silver print.

It is an honor to be working with John again, for he is a man of great nobility and integrity. (Thank you, John.)

Special thanks to the two "Peggys": my business partner, Peggy Denniston, who is always there for quality control, seeing things I don't (for example: "Sheila," she said two days ago, "why don't you reshoot the water fountain at Bienville Square so the stream of water has detail in it—you know, like at a faster shutter speed—so it doesn't look like a blade of Cogon grass reaching into the Gargoyle's mouth?"), and the remarkable Peggy Arnold, extraordinary "angel" and friend, whose wisdom and insight remain a guiding light.

A vigilant setter guards the plot of Stephen Twelves (1861) in Magnolia Cemetery.

I also want to thank my two daughters, Amanda and Kelly Beckham, for understanding that artists have to do what they do and that there is always struggle along the way—and never ever enough money. A thank-you goes to my wonderful little dog, Gracie, for keeping the perennial, ferocious vigil on my front porch, not allowing any other human being or creature to come close to the house except for her people.

Lastly, I want to thank my sister, Sharon Strickland, for restoring my sanity by helping with my complicated tax forms, and my mother, Betty Hagler, whose undying, formidable spirit and love help my daughters and me more than she will ever know.

Sheila Hagler

AN ORNAMENT TO THE CITY

Introduction

Ornamental Cast Iron in American Architecture

Opposite page: Detail, fence, Stephen Twelves plot in Magnolia Cemetery. Victorian Americans fell in love with cast iron's decorative possibilities.

THIS BOOK PRESENTS THE FIRST-EVER ILLUSTRATED, narrative history of Mobile's ornamental ironwork from its nineteenth-century introduction and florescence through its long decline and eventual restoration. It is a colorful story, too long underappreciated, of rawboned iron founders, hustling salesmen, conniving architects, enthusiastic consumers, willful plunderers, romantic artists, and dedicated preservationists. The scholarly and popular inattention to this saga is explained by the incredibly rich ironwork traditions and greater tourism that Charleston, Savannah, and New Orleans have enjoyed. But Mobile has a surprising amount of beautiful and important ironwork too, as well as a remarkably intact and comprehensive historical record that allows a full understanding of how it was manufactured, sold, shipped, and erected at the local level.

Visitors frequently refer to Mobile's historic ironwork as wrought, but the majority of it is cast. Cast iron, cheap and easy to produce in an infinite variety of shapes and designs, captured the imagination of nineteenth-century tastemakers seeking dramatic effect. Virtually every American city accessible by water had some ornamental cast iron, but it was nowhere more exuberantly employed than in the Deep South, particularly the Gulf ports, where wooden structures too rapidly succumbed to the semitropical climate.

Whether locally designed and manufactured or imported from big East Coast foundries, Mobile's nineteenth-century ornamental ironwork nicely exhibits the era's diverse aesthetic tastes. A Greek Revival residential gate, a Gothic-accented cemetery fence, a town house verandah with arabesque patterns—Mobilians' enthusiasm for the practical advantages and decorative delights of these things was no different from that of their countrymen in places like New York, Baltimore, Savannah, Charleston, New Orleans, St. Louis, and sundry smaller river burgs and backcountry hamlets. Therefore, any analysis of Old Mobile ironwork must properly begin with an overview of the larger national story of which it is part and parcel.

Contrasting railings distinguish the Cluis-Rubira House (1857) at 156 St. Anthony Street. A healthy growth of aspidistra, popular since Victorian times and colloquially known as "cast iron plant," sets off the property from the sidewalk.

The Emergence of Ornamental Cast Iron

Man has exploited iron since ancient times (meteorites were an early source), but not until the Industrial Revolution did advancing technology make possible extensive use of the element. Industrial improvements and inventions during the eighteenth century laid the groundwork for the proliferation of ornamental cast iron in the nineteenth century. Most of these innovations took place in England, which was blessed with plenty of iron ore as well as the fuel needed to reduce it to a liquid state.

The British cast iron industry flourished during the late eighteenth and early nineteenth centuries as builders and architects experimented with its structural and ornamental applications. Cast iron bridges were placed over streams, fanciful fences erected around landmarks, and fluted columns used to support church balconies and factory floors, but it was London's wildly popular Crystal Palace, built to house the Great Exhibition of the Industry of All Nations in Hyde Park in 1851, that represented its most stunning use.

America's ironworking technology lagged a few decades behind Britain. Here cities were smaller, trade and transportation networks not as developed, and the general scale of construction less ambitious. The early Republic's iron needs were modest, primarily agricultural and housekeeping related, and adequately served by blacksmiths working at village forges and numerous small foundries. Some wealthy property owners in the cosmopolitan seaports commissioned lovely wrought iron gates, and as early as 1739 there were wrought iron balconies on a few Charleston houses. Eighteenth-century America's ironwork, however, was simple and limited in scope. This began to change in the nineteenth century. Cities grew and became linked by sophisticated water and rail networks, vast iron and coal resources were tapped, industrial capacity exploded, and cast iron emerged as the most useful and versatile material of the age.[1]

Detail, Lyon House porch, 261 N. Joachim Street. Ornamental cast iron's play of light and shadow has long charmed observers.

Early American architects and engineers, many of them British immigrants, employed cast iron for structural and industrial projects just as they had in their homeland, but they also championed its decorative applications. In 1817 in Savannah, architect William Jay added a graceful classical revival cast iron balcony supported on exaggerated acanthus leaf piers to the home of banker and cotton merchant Richard Richardson. This was the first significant use of ornamental cast iron in the South, and Jay was so optimistic for its future that he invested in a nearby foundry. The balcony achieved more fame in 1825, when the Marquis de Lafayette delivered an address from it. In Philadelphia, native-born architect William Strickland provided a cast iron fence featuring an anthemion pattern for the

Wrought Iron, Cast Iron, and Steel

IRON IS AN ABUNDANT NATURAL ELEMENT. ITS THREE MOST common alloys are wrought iron, cast iron, and steel, each determined by the amount of carbon present. Wrought iron contains the least, around .03 percent, and exhibits good tensile strength, which allowed eighteenth-century builders to use it in bridges and as structural beams in buildings. Cast iron has higher carbon content, 3 percent, which makes it harder and good in compression, but brittle and poor in tension. Cast iron's advantages for builders included its resistance to fire and its utility for support columns. Furthermore, the facility of its production ensured its exploitation for repetitive elements and decorative work. Throughout the nineteenth century, wrought and cast elements were satisfactorily combined both structurally (buildings with wrought beams and cast columns) and decoratively (fences with wrought bars and cast finials). Steel, with a carbon content between that of wrought and cast irons, is the strongest of the alloys in tension and compression. Its use did not become widespread until the late nineteenth century when more efficient blast furnaces made it economically feasible, after which it rapidly eclipsed the other alloys in every application.

The production of wrought and cast irons employs pig iron, though in different ways. Pig iron is produced by smelting iron ore in a furnace fired by coke (purified coal). The melted iron is then poured into molds known as sows and pigs (so called for their similarity to a mother pig surrounded by nursing piglets), where it solidifies and the impurities float to the top. To make wrought iron, the pig iron is puddled (reheated and stirred so that the impurities burn off) then further worked down to a residue known as a bloom, a fibrous, malleable mass that can be easily fashioned into a wide array of items. Skilled blacksmiths are capable of breathtakingly beautiful work with wrought iron, but the time and expense required limit its purely decorative uses.

Cast iron production is more complicated and involves three distinct trades—pattern makers, molders, and founders. The pattern makers, usually skilled carpenters, work from drawings to build a wooden copy of the object to be cast, sometimes in multiple sections if large. Next, the molders firmly press the wooden pattern into a sand and clay mixture contained in a wooden box called a flask, then lift it away, leaving a precise imprint. The flask can be open or closed; most ornamental cast iron

Workmen at Mobile Pulley Works tapping out the furnace in preparation for a pour, ca. 1940. This foundry, Mobile's last, closed in 2002. (Courtesy S. Blake McNeely Collection, University of South Alabama Archives.)

pieces are one sided with a rough back, indicating they were cast in an open flask. Next, the founders melt pig iron in a furnace. To harden the soft pig iron, cast scraps are thrown in to increase its carbon content. The golden, molten liquid is poured into the flask through an opening, the sprue, and allowed to cool. When the flask is opened, the sand is brushed away, the sprue scrap is knocked off, and the cast piece is examined for any imperfections. A large, well-managed foundry can produce hundreds of castings a day, but the work is hot, heavy, dirty, and dangerous.

Opposite page: This lovely railing flanks the steps at the Richards House (1860) at 256 N. Joachin Street.

Second Bank of the United States (1821–24) and made use of slender cast iron columns on the three-story porch of the U.S. Naval Asylum (1826–29). John Haviland, a recently arrived British architect, had accurately foreseen matters a few years earlier: "Iron has been applied to many purposes unthought of in former times. The improvement and general introduction of cast iron bids fair to create a totally new school of architecture."[2]

As the century progressed, tastemakers extolled cast iron's virtues in architectural catalogs and pattern books. One of the most influential was Asher Benjamin, who included designs for cast iron balcony railings, window guards, fences, lamps, and verandahs in his 1839 publication *The Builder's Guide*. "The fact that cast iron is produced in most parts of this country," Benjamin wrote, "and at a cost so low as to place it within reach of all . . . and the facility with which it may be wrought into the most beautiful shapes, render it an object worthy of attention here."[3]

Builder-architects and the general public took the cue, and in the decades leading up to the Civil War cast iron building parts like columns, thresholds, window hoods, downspouts, mantels, and staircases and ornamental elements like verandahs, benches, lamps, fences, and gazebos spread far and wide. Iron fencing proved especially popular in rural and small town cemeteries, and cantilevered cast iron balconies adorned the facades of wood-frame southern plantation homes like D'evereux (1840) and Melrose (1845) in Natchez and the Knox House (1848) in Montgomery.[4]

Styles and Patterns

As in other aspects of the antebellum American decorative arts, the dominant stylistic influences on ornamental cast iron were the Greek Revival (1820–70), Picturesque/Rustic (post-1850), Gothic Revival (1840–70), and Italianate (1850–80), all more or less overlapping midcentury. A Greek Revival balcony or fence might feature any number of motifs—a lyre, a lotus, an urn, anthemion cresting, acanthus leaf accents, or a Greek key border. Picturesque/Rustic themes include all kinds of natural flora such as vines, grape clusters, flowers, oak branches, and leaves, often intricately intertwined. Gothic Revival elements, particularly popular on cemetery fences, include crockets, trefoils, and quatrefoils. Italianate town homes in Mobile and New Orleans exhibit elaborate floral verandahs, some accented with allegorical figures, the better to create the appearance of a country villa.

This beautiful arabesque on the Richards House illustrates ornamental cast iron's artistic possibilities.

The Emergence of Robert Wood

Cast iron's transcendence was made possible by the visionary and aggressive schemes of foundry men like Robert Wood of Philadelphia, a marketing genius who was by no means unique to the trade. Born in 1813 and at an early age apprenticed to a blacksmith, Wood went into business for himself in 1839, specializing in simple wrought iron building components. Pennsylvania's rich coalfields and excellent canal system made the state a natural location for iron foundries, and by 1849 Wood owned one, calling his business "Robert Wood, Iron Rail Foundry and Manufacturing." That same year, he printed and distributed a profusely illustrated, free catalog showcasing his products, *Wood's Portfolio of Original Designs of Iron Railings, Verandahs,*

Settees, Chairs, Tables and Other Ornamental and Architectural Iron. He was one of the first businessmen in American history to publish such a catalog, and the public responded enthusiastically.[5]

The firm's reputation grew to the point that, in 1853, C. T. Hinckley, a writer for *Godey's Lady's Book*, made a special visit and penned an extensive, fact-filled account, "A Day at the Ornamental Iron Works of Robert Wood." After providing some general historical background on the iron industry, Hinckley detailed his "day of unbounded gratification and instruction" on the factory's premises. He walked his readers through the entire casting process, beginning with the pattern room, where he discovered workmen busily making wooden models. He then described how the molders would press each model into a flask, "and tramp upon it with their feet until it is compact." In the casting area, he thrilled to the sight of the molten iron as it poured out of the cupola, throwing off "the most beautiful sparkles, which fly around in every direction, emitting a light of great brilliancy." Scurrying workmen filled their ladles, making pours into the flasks scattered about the foundry floor. From these dramatic activities Hinckley passed into the finishing rooms, which presented "a scene of beauty, bustle, and noise" as the "almost endless" varieties of ornamental ironwork were given their final polish and prepared for shipping by sea or rail. At the end of his article Hinckley confessed, "We have given but a general idea of the varieties of uses to which cast-iron has been applied. Were we to enumerate the various sizes and styles of vases, cemetery railings, &c. &c., it would exceed the space which we have at command. Of the railing alone we saw over one hundred and fifty patterns."[6] Something of the American appetite for ornamental iron may be fathomed from the fact that Wood's foundry was one of more than twenty in Philadelphia alone, with significant other operations in New York, Boston, Baltimore, and many other cities.[7]

Wood was a tough and effective competitor in a ruthless trade. Nineteenth-century foundries ceaselessly conspired against one another and routinely pirated designs (there was no patent protection then). Some marked their finished pieces, but most did not, making a determination of the original source virtually impossible. Identification was further complicated because roving, free-agent designers sold their sketches to multiple firms and because thriving firms marketed as their own designs acquired from failing houses. Wood took innovative steps to improve his edge in this environment. He formed a partnership in 1857 with a talented designer, Elliston

Perot, continued issuing handsome catalogs, and established a branch operation in New Orleans known as Wood, Miltenberger & Co. In addition, he created profitable agencies in cities like Mobile, supplying his representatives with catalogs and price lists and occasionally visiting them to promote the trade. His firm's success was staggering: by 1878 its products, many of them marked, were in thirty of the thirty-eight states. Among its high-profile commissions was President James Monroe's tomb (1859), a canopied, twelve-foot-high cagelike confection in Richmond's Hollywood Cemetery that still elicits gasps. Despite his achievements, however, Wood struggled with high overhead (he employed three hundred hands in 1878), continued merciless competition, and declining demand, all of which forced him to declare bankruptcy in 1881. He died five years later. By then, ornamental cast iron's heyday was over.[8]

Opposite page: Gallery detail, Silver House (1845), 257 St. Francis Street. A rare type with its raised first story deck and steps, this gallery is nicely adapted to its urban context.

Porches and Balconies

Though everyday Americans uncritically embraced the myriad manifestations of ornamental ironwork, they were especially fond of those that provided shelter from sun and rain. These were variously and imprecisely labeled porches, piazzas, galleries, verandahs, or porticos on residences, and balconies, verandahs, or galleries on commercial buildings. Architects were cognizant of the technicalities—a verandah was agreed to be roofed, for example—but most people didn't care and used whatever term appealed. In the Deep South, *verandah* was by far the favorite.[9]

Both tastemakers and the general public enthused over the delights of cast iron residential porches. In *The Model Architect* (1852), Samuel Sloan endorsed the "growing taste for porches and verandahs" and recommended iron columns for support.[10] Artists and writers in particular were much taken with the romantic image of foliage-choked verandahs. In her 1854 novel *Fashion and Famine*, Ann S. Stevens waxed lyrical over a New York cottage with "netted ironwork that hung around the doors, the windows, and fringed the eaves, as it were, with a valance of massive lace . . . luxuriously interwoven with creeping plants."[11]

The multitiered cast iron balconies that crowded the downtowns of southern cities like Savannah, Mobile, and especially New Orleans provoked the most comment, then as now. Not surprisingly, it was a New Orleans building that boasted one of the first of these immensely useful adaptations. The Verandah Hotel, erected at St. Charles and Common streets by the relocated New York architects James and

Charles Dakin in 1836, featured a cantilevered iron balcony wrapping two sides of the building, covered by a separate canopy supported on iron columns all the way out to the sidewalk's edge. According to James Dakin's biographer, Arthur Scully, an architectural historian and Crescent City resident, the Verandah Hotel "led to a craze for cast iron balconies. Pretty soon you saw balconies popping up all over not only in the American Sector, where the Verandah Hotel was located, but in the French Quarter as well."[12] The Verandah remained a prominent landmark and popular watering hole until it was destroyed by fire in 1855.[13]

The practical advantages of these full balconies in Gulf Coast cities, alternately drenched by tropical downpours and steamed by fierce sun, were manifold. Downtown pedestrians could walk for blocks beneath them without being exposed to the elements. The second and, in some cases, third levels, if protected, offered shady repose to residents and office workers and provided a handy perch during Mardi Gras parades. In 1852 the *New Orleans Daily Picayune* applauded the trend: "One of the most admirable innovations upon the old system of building tall, staring structures for business purposes, is the plan which we are glad to see is generally coming into use, of erecting galleries and verandahs of ornamental ironwork."[14]

With an eager public, an enthusiastic press, a booming economy, and several iron foundries, including Wood, Miltenberger & Co., New Orleans blossomed with ornamental ironwork of all kinds. As early as the 1870s, travelers began to comment on it and local colorists to romanticize it, years earlier than was the case for most other southern cities. In his travelogue *The Great South* (1879), Edward King detailed the French Quarter's old-world flavor: "The houses are all of stucco or brick stuccoed or painted, the windows of each story descend to the floors, opening like doors, upon airy, pretty balconies, protected by iron railings."[15] George Washington Cable, whose collection *Old Creole Days* (1879) painted the city as a culture apart, chose to celebrate the decay, which was an aspect of the Quarter even then. It was, he wrote, "a region of architectural decrepitude, where an ancient and foreign-seeming domestic life, in second stories, overhangs the ruins of former commercial prosperity." Most of the balconies, he reported, were "begrimed and rust-eaten," which for him only increased their allure.[16]

Cast Iron Buildings and Facades

Far from the sunny South, capacious balconies made little sense, but cast iron structures and facades did, and in big cities like New York, Baltimore, and Chicago (and to a lesser degree in the South), iron facades and, more rarely, entire buildings became all the rage. Cast iron's ornamental and structural qualities combined beautifully in these applications. Its strength permitted increased building height (up to five or six stories) and larger openings, and its fire resistance was a plus in densely built commercial districts. These facades were the forerunners of steel-frame skyscrapers and prefabricated building elements. Mid-nineteenth-century architects were pleased by both the practical and decorative possibilities, store owners found the larger window openings advantageous for display and greater light, and the public was dazzled by the ornamental wizardry along cornices and around windows. Many facades featured complex combinations of classical columns, brackets, and dentil work that gave the buildings a strong Venetian feel.

Just as the New Orleans press endorsed the spread of balconies, the northern press hailed cast iron architecture. In 1852, the *Philadelphia Public Ledger* helped its readers imagine the construction of such an edifice: "Some carts would arrive with beautiful cast iron blocks, and a few men with derrick, block and tackle, would be seen quietly hoisting these blocks and fitting them into their places, and perhaps by evening . . . a building, which would endure for ages, will be seen standing erect, in dignity and beauty." James Bogardus, a New York builder whose 1849 Edward

Opposite page: These cast iron verandahs on the Frolichstein House (foreground) and Goldsmith House seem almost to dance with the trees. Located at 337–59 Church Street, they have intrigued passersby since the Civil War.

Laing store was one of the earlier examples of cast iron architecture, wrote an evangelistic treatise on the subject. In the 1856 publication *Cast Iron Buildings: Their Construction and Advantages*, Bogardus declared that not only would such structures "tend to elevate the public taste" but they would also "endure a thousand years."[17]

Not everyone was on the cast iron bandwagon, however, including some prominent members of the architectural establishment. In 1848, the English critic and writer John Ruskin, who had an audience on both sides of the Atlantic, fussily dismissed iron for architectural purposes. "No ornaments," he wrote, "are so cold, clumsy, and vulgar, so essentially incapable of a fine line, or a shadow, as those of cast iron."[18] In America, Andrew Jackson Downing, whose writings on gardens and rural cottages greatly influenced public taste, harshly condemned the widespread "exhibition of ironmongery" so evident in cemeteries.[19] Neither writer found much sympathy for these views, however.

The Civil War dampened the ornamental use of cast iron, as foundries North and South turned their efforts to military production. In the spring of 1862, the *New Orleans Daily Delta* informed its readers that one local operation, once bent on architectural projects, had been forced to direct its attention "to the preparation of munitions of war, and now you will see in their extensive establishment any quantity of shot and shell."[20] Cast iron was also used on warships and in the Confederate submarine *Hunley*, which was fabricated in a Mobile foundry.[21] Looming over the nation as a reminder of cast iron's more constructive possibilities was the unfinished dome of the U.S. Capitol in Washington.

With peace, the public's appetite for ornamental ironwork returned. Even in the occupied southern coastal cities, construction activity was lively enough to insure steady demand. Foundries proliferated nationwide, many imitating Wood's prewar experiment with catalogs. In the late 1870s, a writer for *The Manufacturer and Builder* magazine visited the warehouse of J. W. Fiske, a New York iron founder. He compared it to an art gallery and ticked off the thirty catalogs available: "1st, illustrated catalogue of fountains, 100 pages, folio size; 2d, of vases, with 120 different forms; 3d, of weather vanes and crosses for church spires; 4th, of iron railings, columns, etc.; 5th iron wire fences and railings for banks and offices" and so on.[22] No one would have been surprised, and few would have disagreed, when foundry owner Edward Kirk dubbed iron "the symbol of civilization" in his 1877 book *The Founding Metals*.

Detail, cast iron bench, Convent of the Visitation.

Out of Vogue

Only a few years after Kirk's pronouncement, however, the world shifted, and steel emerged as the universal building material. Though ornamental ironwork would remain popular through the turn of the century, the future belonged to steel. Changing aesthetic values further insured iron's decline.

From the 1880s to the 1930s, American cities burgeoned, their skylines defined by steel-framed high-rise buildings. Ornament and ostentation fell from favor, but the older cast iron fences, lampposts, facades, and balconies—some well maintained, others deteriorating—remained on the landscape as reminders of the past.

Opposing attitudes toward these decorative leftovers soon developed. On one side were nascent preservationists—amateur local historians, photographers, writers, and painters for the most part, especially well represented in the southern seaports—

Railing detail, McCoy House, 253 State Street. Both homeowners and tourists have long delighted in the interplay of foliage and ironwork.

who were charmed by the old ironwork and romanticized it in little publications and newspaper sketches. Arrayed against them were politicians, civic boosters, and architects who viewed the old iron as passé at best and an embarrassing eyesore at worst.

Unfortunately, by the 1930s the latter view was reinforced by a robust international scrap iron market. Opportunistic junk dealers swept through America's cities, buying up all they could get; whether old boilers or lacy garden gates, it mattered not to them. Much of the demand was driven by Imperial Japan, whose war machine was sweeping through China and the Pacific. When Congress finally banned sales of scrap to that country in October 1940, many cities had already been stripped of tons of ornamental ironwork. Most of the balconies along Canal Street in New Orleans were gone, and losses were also great in nearby Mobile. More than one thoughtful observer feared dire consequences if war was declared. Only days before the Pearl Harbor attack, a New York labor leader predicted, "Well, that scrap iron is going to start flying back at us any day now."[23] After the United States entered World War II, ornamental ironwork that hadn't already been plundered was endangered by patriotic scrap drives. Among the more tragic losses was the Richard Upjohn-designed fence surrounding Boston Common.[24]

Preservationists to the Rescue

By the 1960s and 1970s, historic preservation efforts became better organized and more effective. In New York City, Margot Gayle, a tireless worker, established the Friends of Cast Iron Architecture in 1970. Shrewdly, Gayle anchored her board with a distinguished list of city elites. The Friends surveyed Gotham's surviving ironwork and established recognition and legal protection through landmark designations. Historic districts were created in many other cities as well, including New Orleans and Mobile, and ornamental ironwork was used to market tourism and historic homes tours. Even in small towns and rural areas, historic societies and citizen groups banded together to protect cemetery ironwork and isolated landmarks. As downtowns were revitalized throughout the Deep South, cast iron balconies once more came into favor as valued amenities on commercial buildings, and foundry owners discovered new life in their dusty old patterns.[25]

Old Mobile's cast iron reflects this broader national picture in most respects. But it is also a fascinating story in its own right, both uplifting and heartbreaking, never before told in full.

Chapter One

Flowering

Mobile Iron to 1861

Opposite page: The Richards House is dramatically demarcated from the sidewalk by one of the best-preserved cast iron residential fences in the city.

MOBILE'S FIRST IRONWORKER WAS A FRENCH blacksmith, his name now lost to history. He labored in a small timber and mud structure on the western fringes of the original 1702 settlement at Twenty-seven Mile Bluff. Recent archaeological investigations inside the smithy have uncovered large quantities of slag and coal, as well as iron rods and scrap. This evidence proves that, like most other blacksmiths in early America, this Frenchman concentrated on practical rather than decorative projects—making nails, hinges, and gun parts and repairing weapons and tools.[1]

Throughout Mobile's century-long colonial period these applications remained the most important manifestations of the ironworker's art. French, then British, and then Spanish blacksmiths sweated over anvils and forges, hammering out horseshoes, wagon fittings, blades, and other necessities. Because the town was not prosperous—it largely consisted of modest one-story frame buildings surrounded by rickety wooden palings—there was no need for fancy iron gates or balconies.[2]

After the Americans acquired Mobile in 1813, the situation remained roughly the same for a time. The most important ironworker during this period was John J.

The Lyon House verandah (1860) mixes disparate patterns in riotous excess. Lacy brackets, drop friezes, and pendants dazzle the eye, but this verandah lacks the cosmopolitan coherence of the Richards House just across the street. Note that the railing pattern abutting the left, first-story column does not match that on the other side of the steps or above. Ornamental ironwork became popular as early as the 1830s.

Glidden, an English machinist and blacksmith who came to the Port City via St. Stephens around 1816. Glidden set up a large smithy on Royal Street downtown and trained his slaves in the craft. As in the colonial era the work focused on the manufacture and repair of utilitarian household and agricultural objects. One significant difference was the increased emphasis on riverboat work, some of it heavy and difficult, involving boilers and large pieces of machinery. As the nineteenth century progressed, local ironworkers found steady work building, maintaining, and repairing steamboats and trains. Decorative work, though hardly negligible by midcentury, would never be a mainstay.[3]

Mobile's fortunes improved with Alabama's statehood in 1819 and the subsequent settlement of the Black Belt and Mississippi prairie. The city's wharves bustled with shipping, and residents constructed homes, businesses, and public buildings, many of brick. In parallel, the iron trade grew in scope and complexity. By 1833 the town had at least one foundry, operated by Asa Prior. In a newspaper ad Prior boasted that his establishment was "in successful operation under the management of an experienced founder." He promised that all orders would be "faithfully executed with dispatch" and offered cash for scrap iron, copper, and brass.[4]

For reasons now unknown, Prior's business folded shortly thereafter. The trade clearly held promise, however, as demonstrated by Isaac D. Spear and William Alderson, an energetic pair of ironworkers who formed a partnership in 1836 and contracted to erect a new foundry on Water Street, near the river. Spear, a native Pennsylvanian, and Alderson, an Englishman, knew their business and carefully detailed exactly how they wanted their foundry constructed. The building was to be a three-story brick edifice forty-five feet wide by thirty-six feet deep with an attached molding shed and "two Chimnies of suitable highth & size to carry off smoke from Furnace & Engine." Plans also called for wooden support columns throughout the interior, numerous windows, and large double doors with a hoisting tackle above.[5]

ISAAC D. SPEAR & CO.
CONSTRUCT PLAIN AND ORNAMENTAL
Iron Railing, and House Work
OF ALL DESCRIPTIONS.
BANK DOORS, BOOK CASES,
IRON WINDOW-FRAMES AND SHUTTERS,
Ship and Steam Engine Work,
Sawmill, Machine and Brass Foundry work
OF ALL KINDS, CAST, TURNED AND FINISHED;
AS WELL AS JOBBING AND SMITH'S WORK
in all its branches, in a most workmanlike manner, on their premises, in
Water street, opposite Col. Matthew's Steam Press,
BETWEEN CHURCH AND THEATRE STREETS,
MOBILE.

Isaac D. Spear & Co. advertisement from Mobile City Directory, *1837.*

The business, initially known as Isaac D. Spear & Co. and later renamed the Phoenix Foundry, advertised a wide range of services including "Ship and Steam Engine work, Sawmill, Machine and Brass Foundry work of all kinds, cast, turned and finished as well as jobbing and smith's work in all its branches." Significantly, the foundry also offered "plain and ornamental iron railing," the first local ironworks to do so. The complexity and size of the Phoenix Foundry may be appreciated by the fact that on the eve of the Civil War it employed twenty-eight men—including an architect, two finishers, ten machinists, three blacksmiths, five pattern makers, two foremen, two boilermakers, two molders, and a carpenter.[6]

The Phoenix was not without competition during the antebellum years, most notably from Skates & Co. (also known as Mobile Foundry). The principals of this firm, Charles W. Gazzam and B. F. Skates, were experienced founders with Pennsylvania roots. Like Spear and Alderson at the Phoenix, they specialized in heavy work with steam engines, as well as cotton gins and sawmills. In 1861 they had

Detail from the Goodwin and Haire map, 1824. This cotton warehouse, long since destroyed, featured one of the earliest iron balconies in the Port City.

eighteen employees, ten of them machinists, and did $150,000 worth of business annually.[7]

Besides large foundries like the Phoenix and Skates, numerous independent blacksmiths and whitesmiths (tin and sheet metal workers) serviced the town, and several of them could do small-scale ornamental projects. Among these craftsmen was John Lang, who, in an all too rare practice, actually marked his work. A cast iron cemetery gate stamped "J. LANG, MAKER" and featuring a pair of lambs and a willow tree is now at the Museum of Mobile.[8]

All of Mobile's ironworks, large or small, were dependent on imported raw materials, mostly from Pennsylvania and Scotland. This riled local boosters. The *Mobile Advertiser* grumbled that "the inexhaustible beds of ore in Alabama" should have been the source.[9] But such would not be the case until after the ornamental ironwork fad passed.

Ironworking was a profitable business for entrepreneurs like Alderson, Spear, Skates, and Gazzam, and they enjoyed public approval and acclaim. But for the men who actually labored on the foundry floor, tending the furnaces, pouring the molten iron, and wrestling the castings loose from heavy flasks, the work was backbreaking and gritty. Still, these men earned wages and could look forward to a Saturday night carouse. For the slaves who often worked alongside them, however, the rewards were meager.

Fascinating and rare insight into the life of an enslaved ironworker is provided by the autobiography of John P. Parker, who worked in several Mobile foundries during the 1840s. Parker eventually bought his freedom, moved to Ohio, and, during the 1880s, dictated his story to a newspaper reporter. According to his account, he was born in Norfolk, Virginia, in 1827 and brought to Mobile when he was eight. His owner, a physician, was a kindly man who wanted him to master a trade. Therefore, when Parker was a teenager, he was placed in a foundry (most likely the Phoenix) to learn how to be a molder. "Being of an inventive turn of mind," he told the reporter, "I soon rigged up my bench so I could do more and better work than any man in the shop." Unfortunately, this caused resentment among Parker's white coworkers and soon enough real trouble. One day, the superintendent ordered Parker to help him with a large casting, and when Parker put him off, a confrontation ensued. Words escalated until, Parker recalled, "The next thing I knew, I was in a regular knock-down-and-drag-out fistfight." He was subsequently sold and went to work in another foundry, where his wages were applied toward his freedom. But Parker again found that his industriousness led to difficulties and fights. His resentment over this remained strong all his life. "I hated the injustices and restraints against my own initiative," he fumed. "To me that was the great curse of slavery."[10]

Mobile's first balconies were cantilevered, wrought iron affairs with modest scroll-work like this one, a late example of the type, on the Elkus House (1854) at 50 S. Franklin Street.

With so many talented ironworkers, a vigorous port, a warm climate, and growing public interest, Mobile's embrace of ornamental ironwork was inevitable. The first example of it can no longer be determined, though it might have been as early as 1822, when a large brick cotton warehouse with a cantilevered iron balcony was erected at Royal and Conti streets. Three years later the Duke of Saxe-Weimar Eisenach, a German aristocrat who was traveling the country, wrote that of all the buildings in Mobile, this one "most excited my attention."[11] A good picture of it graces the left margin of the 1824 Goodwin and Haire map, which shows the balcony's woven wire panels between heavy square balusters with a decorative top border. Whether this balcony was locally manufactured or imported is unknown, though probably the latter.[12]

The Emanuel House (1836, demolished 1936), designed by James Gallier. This sophisticated town home's ironwork exhibited numerous classical motifs typical of antebellum Mobile. Note especially the anthemion crests and lyres in the railing over the portico. (Courtesy George B. Rogers Collection, University of South Alabama Archives.)

Balconies made good sense in Mobile's sultry air, and wooden ones had been popular for years. But the advantages of iron were obvious, and surviving building contracts confirm that locals enthusiastically embraced it during the 1830s. City fathers attempted to regulate matters in the code, which stated that "no gallery, balcony or other projection . . . shall in future be made to extend or project over any street more than five feet, nor in any manner at a less height than twelve feet above the sidewalks or footways." Furthermore, the code disallowed "posts or pillars" as supports because they might interfere with the activities of the wagons, buggies, drays, and pedestrians that typically crowded local curbs. Violators faced a five-dollar-a-day fine and removal of the offending balcony. Given these restrictions, Mobile's earliest iron balconies were simple cantilevered affairs supported on plain brackets. The railings featured small, square wrought iron uprights, C-curve spacers, and sometimes a minimally decorative top band with scrollwork or elongated S-curves positioned on their sides.[13]

A typical reference to an iron balcony occurs in a contract dated May 24, 1831, between John K. Collins and Charles Barney for a three-story brick building to be erected on Commerce Street, along the riverfront. In the document, Collins, the builder, promised to "procure, find and provide all stone, brick, timber, iron, copper, slating" necessary to complete the job. This did not include, however, "the iron gallery or galleries," that Barney was to supply at his own expense. A clearer picture of an iron balcony, though not a common type, is provided in the contract signed August 12, 1839, for a new county jail, also to be constructed by Collins. The jail was to feature three-story cellblocks with attached balconies surrounding an exercise yard. According to the contract, the balconies were to be "two feet wide on three sides and four feet wide on the other side" and "stretch around the second and third stories of the Granite cells with a flight of Steps two feet wide supported by Iron horses [metal equivalents to wooden sawhorses] leading up to each story." This was a sturdy, utilitarian apparatus, devoid of any decorative elements and not meant to be seen by the public.[14]

If the contracts are any indication though, by the 1840s, cantilevered iron balconies were fairly common downtown. The way was prepared, and within just a few short years a sea change in popular taste would overthrow the code, transforming how Mobile would be perceived for more than a century.

Balconies were not the only examples of the ironworker's art downtown. Beginning in 1834, cast iron posts were employed for the gas lamps illuminating city streets. Most were fluted or faceted poles topped with a wide crosspiece and the lantern itself, usually copper. The city purchased the lamps as needed while the gas company kept them maintained and lit. Each evening a lamplighter made his rounds, placed his ladder against each post's crosspiece, climbed aloft, opened the glass, and lit the lantern by hand. To keep costs down, a schedule of "lighting by the moon" was followed until 1877, after which the lamps were kept lit all night. The press occasionally clamored for more lamps, as in the autumn of 1859, when the *Mobile Daily Register* recommended that Bienville Square be better illuminated. The paper argued that the increased lighting would "exclude from the decent female society who may assemble there, those of that class who are not allowed to mingle with them in other places." The city responded to such appeals to the best of its ability, and by 1864 more than two hundred lamps had been installed downtown. Maintenance proved to be a constant headache, however, what with trigger-happy vandals shooting out the glass and wayward carriages smashing into the poles with enough regularity to suggest the city fathers' probable wisdom in forbidding sidewalk balcony supports. Despite these difficulties, Mobile's iron lampposts were conscientiously looked after, and several survive to this day.[15]

This graceful gate and fence at Henry Hitchcock's plot (1839) in Magnolia Cemetery combine wrought and cast iron to lovely effect. The pointed pickets, C-spacers, and paired lyres are wrought, while the fluted posts, anthemion crests, and picket collars are cast.

Fences and gates were another important use of iron, and they were soon much in evidence downtown as well as in Church Street Graveyard and Magnolia Cemetery. Among the first and most impressive to be erected were the monumental gates and fence surrounding Barton Academy on Government Street. Barton Academy, constructed in 1836 as a public school, was designed by the architects James Gallier

and James Dakin. Their plans called for a massive Greek Revival edifice capped by a columned rotunda. As construction proceeded, the building committee made certain that the school would be appropriately framed and set off from the street. On October 15 it voted to take bids "for an iron fence, gates, & etc., with a brick and granite base for the same."[16] Robert E. Redwood, a local iron manufacturer, submitted the low bid of $4,000. The committee's minutes indicate that the fence was ordered from New York, though the exact source is not named. Upon erection, the result was elegant and appropriately symbolic. The main double gates, flanked by smaller scale pedestrian gates, consist of wrought iron bars with cast spear points and are hinged on eleven-foot-high paneled cast iron piers with palmette appliqués and floral finials. The fence palings, matching the gate bars, are spaced at intervals of fifteen by posts cast as Roman fasces (bundles of sticks bound by leather and symbolizing authority).[17]

Above: This fence at the William Crawford plot (1849) in Magnolia Cemetery exhibits a simple Greek key motif along its bottom border. The design is thought to be a reference to the labyrinthine Minotaur's lair of ancient mythology.

Opposite page: The gates and fence at Barton Academy (1836), 504 Government Street, are an elegant manifestation of neoclassicism in iron. Wrought iron railings with scrolled top border decorate the columned portico of the building itself.

With its palmettes and fasces, the Barton fence presents a good high-style example of classicism's early nineteenth-century dominance in the Port City. Other Greek-inspired motifs to be found on early fences and balconies include anthemion cresting, acanthus leaves, Greek key borders, and lyres. A visitor to Mobile in 1845 would have found its ironwork to be clean, symmetrical, and proportional—restrained almost—a decided complement to the streetscape. Change was coming, however, heralded by a petition.

"To the Honorable Boards of Mayor, Aldermen and Common Council," it began. "Your petitioners respectfully request permission to erect over their side walks, verandahs according to such plan as may be recommended and adopted by you." The plea was dated October 24, 1848, and signed by forty-one individuals, all downtown merchants, mostly located along Royal, Water, Commerce, and Dauphin streets. They included Antonio Philips, a restaurateur; John C. Peters and Jacque Leforts, grocers; George Schumacher, a confectioner; and Joseph Roderiquez, a barkeep, as well as ship chandlers, commission merchants, and a justice of the peace. What they wanted were full, roofed balconies extending to the sidewalk's edge, supported by

Opposite page: An example of the Port City's most beautiful ornamental ironwork, the Slatter Mausoleum (1860) and its surrounding Gothic Revival fence in Magnolia Cemetery were ordered by a cotton factor. The pieces arrived undamaged in forty heavily packed wooden boxes.

columns or posts. These would be much wider than the cantilevered ones that were then the rule, and the supports would constitute a potential impediment to passersby. The merchants realized their request was contrary to the city code but offered to pay an annual fee for the privilege, "thereby increasing the revenues of the City of Mobile."[18] The city referred the matter to committee, which reported back several weeks later. In its assessment, the committee stated its belief that if the petition were granted, the resulting gaggle of verandahs would "impair if not destroy the beauty and symmetry of the city, and greatly injure the comfort and convenience of the public streets." Furthermore, the committee argued that "it would be an uncommon innovation upon the usages of other cities, and ought not to be hazarded but upon perfect confidence of right and well grounded assurances of public utility." The administration concurred and the petition was denied.[19]

Despite official resistance, however, the merchants soon got their way, probably by persistence and sheer weight of numbers. Though no official retraction appears in the records, soon enough the code reflected the new reality, allowing balconies to extend out and requiring that the supports "be composed of iron, and placed on a line within four inches of the outer line of the curb of the side-walk." In the same section, officials also addressed another sidewalk application of cast iron that had become quite common and limited hitching posts to five feet in height.[20]

Two years after the petition King Cotton was firmly enthroned in the Deep South, and Mobile emerged as one of the busiest ports in the nation. "A new era of prosperity is beginning to dawn," crowed *Rowan's Directory*, "and a bright prospect to the Mobilian, is in full view."[21] Cotton exports increased dramatically, peaking at more than 680,000 bales in 1856. The city's population increased to nearly 30,000, roughly a third slaves, and commercial and residential construction exploded. A French traveler to the Port City remarked that one "would need only to stroll briefly through its main thoroughfares and especially along its wharves in order to observe there the extraordinary business activity evident on all sides."[22]

This increased prosperity dovetailed nicely with the public's growing interest in ornamental ironwork, and a few quick-thinking men hastened to establish relationships with large northern foundries to capitalize on the possibilities. Among them were Alderson at the Phoenix Foundry, who served as an agent for Moore & Gallagher Ornamental Ironworks, a Philadelphia concern, and T. S. James, a local architect who represented Chase, Brother & Co. of Boston. By far the most effective was Thomas

Opposite page: The gates (1860) at the Cathedral of the Immaculate Conception, 4 S. Claiborne Street, communicate the property's ecclesiastical function through various symbols. These include the crosses atop the posts, the trefoils along the bottom border, and the wreathed "AM" motifs at the center of each gate, which signify Ave Maria.

Ellison, a cotton broker who became the agent for Robert Wood's Philadelphia Ironworks in 1852. Working closely with his sponsor, Ellison proved to be a strong competitor, and during the ten years he held the agency, Wood's ironwork dominated the market. Ellison maintained an office in the heart of Mobile's booming waterfront at Commerce and Conti streets, where he kept catalogs and price lists for customers to browse. He placed their orders, handled the shipping, and took an agent's fee of 10 percent. In an 1854 newspaper ad, he enumerated the many varieties of cast iron available, including settees, chairs, hat and umbrella stands, greyhounds, lions, fountains, urns, and ornamental work "adapted to PRIVATE and PUBLIC BUILDINGS."[23]

That meant verandahs, which were fast coming into their prime. One of Ellison's earliest commissions was for the cast iron balcony on the Battle House Hotel, constructed in 1852 at the southeast corner of Royal and St. Francis streets. Boston architect Isaiah Rogers designed the 240-room, four-story brick hostelry, which featured a palatial restaurant and bar. The *Mobile Daily Register* was especially pleased with plans for the accompanying ironwork, writing on September 28, "The Verandah will not be less ornamental than useful to the establishment. Without it, the house would look more like a cotton factory than the splendid hotel it is, and the lady dwellers within could never get a peep outside at the barbarians even when the military paraded by day, or the far famed 'Cobellions' at night."[24] Almost three months later, after the verandah had been attached, the paper gushed that the hotel "seemed like some Fairy Palace, which had sprung up in the heart of our city."[25] The Battle House quickly became Mobile's premier inn and a social crossroads, and the verandah proved to be such a popular feature that in 1870 it was replaced by a still larger one wrapping two elevations.[26]

Ellison scored another significant commission later in the decade with an order for a fence and gates at Bienville Square. His impromptu addition of some cast iron statuary further enhanced this public space. Acquired by the city in 1824 and bounded by Dauphin, St. Joseph, St. Francis, and Conception streets, the square was substantially improved during the fifteen years leading up to the Civil War. In 1847 ranks of oak trees were planted (now grown to magnificent proportions) and broad walkways installed. Plans also called for a fence to surround the entire square, with gates at each corner. Though Ellison won the bid in 1854, the nearly $10,000 had to be privately raised. Efforts included a benefit concert by the Lake Minstrels at a dollar a ticket and several large individual donations.[27] Even so, the fund-raising

Above: Sambo. Moved four times in response to shifting political winds, this statue has at last found peace outside Mobile's National African American Archives, 564 Martin Luther King Jr. Avenue. Once a standard catalog item, only a few still exist nationwide.

Opposite page: The iron deer in Washington Square, prior to its 2004 restoration.

took several years. At last, in 1858, the new fence and gates were installed, and the *Mobile Daily Register* took especial pride in the fact that "this ornament has been the result of public spirit on the part of our citizens."[28] The massive fence was not a success with the public that funded it, however. People found it an inconvenient impediment, and it was removed in 1889, after which it was quickly forgotten. Not so the two statues that Ellison put on the low mound in the square's center. These pieces proved to be very popular indeed. From the moment they were set down, each began a long and strange odyssey, one coming to embody neighborhood pride and childhood delight, the other racial tensions and conflict.[29]

They were a cast iron buck deer and a Negro slave boy. In a charming tableau, the boy held onto the deer by a small chain. There is no record of the city ordering or paying for these pieces, nor does any correspondence survive from Ellison regarding their acquisition. Based on later correspondence from Ellison's successor as well as local folklore, an educated guess can be made as to how they came to rest in the square. Concurrent with the other improvements, Ellison decided to request the statues as an advertisement of Wood's products. Just who owned them was subsequently to be the subject of some confusion, but Wood probably did and simply loaned them to further Ellison's agency. As far as the mayor and common council were concerned, the pieces were an attractive, and free, complement to the city.[30]

Deer were popular icons in Victorian England and America. Inspired by Prince Albert's love of the hunt, images of noble stags and peaceful deer were seemingly everywhere, from paintings and engravings to silver, china, and fabrics. By the late 1840s, cast iron representations of these animals began to appear on grassy swards North and South, and virtually every foundry worth its salt made them. Ellison's choice of an iron deer to enhance Mobile's public square was well within the mainstream of mid-nineteenth-century taste and made perfect sense.[31]

The slave boy or groom, referred to as Sambo, was also a popular image. Shrewd businessman that he was, Wood no doubt saw a cast iron replica as highly marketable in the slave states. The statue is anything but a caricature, however. The boy's visage is sympathetically rendered, and he appears wistful, as if contemplating his condition. A single suspender holds up his trousers, and his shirt is torn and loose.

Chris

He stands barefoot on a cotton bale, his right arm bent, a large ring in hand. Though Sambo was obviously meant to serve as a hitching post, Ellison chose to place him with the deer. Combinations of children and animals were also common in American art, and passersby no doubt found the pairing touching and sweet. This innocent beginning for Sambo and his pet deer gave little hint of the difficult days ahead.[32]

Ellison's agency was extraordinarily successful. Mobile's business and professional elites enthusiastically placed their orders with him, and over the course of the 1850s the city bloomed with Robert Wood's productions. Prominent and still extant examples include the Perrine fence and Slatter mausoleum in Magnolia Cemetery, the elaborate fence and gates at the Cathedral of the Immaculate Conception on Claiborne Street (supplied by Wood and Miltenberger of New Orleans), the two-story verandah at the Guesnard House on Jackson Street and, most spectacular of all, the exuberant allegorical verandah at the Richards House on Joachim Street.

Capable and hardworking as he was, Ellison did not have a lock on the trade. Other foundries, both northern and local, also won commissions. Among these was the New York Wire Railing Works, which advertised "Window Guards and Gratings for Stores, Dwellings, Lunatic Asylums, Prisons, etc."[33] Represented by a local blacksmith named William Rouse, this company supplied the exquisite woven wire lunettes on the Italianate-style city hall and market, built in 1856. The contract required that the ironwork "be good, workmanlike and elegant" and cost at least $3,500. The contractor recommended Rouse to city officials, stating, "his estimate is over 3500 and he is an honest man and will do as good and faithful a job as any." The results pleased the Joint Committee on Public Property, which reported that the new municipal building and its sinuous ironwork were "an ornament to the city."[34]

D. D. Badger and Co. of New York supplied Mobile's first cast iron building facade in 1860 for the Daniels, Elgin and Company, a dry goods establishment at the foot of Dauphin Street. The merchants selected this novelty themselves, rather than

Opposite page and above: The Richards House (1860), an Italianate mansion, represents cast iron's apogee in Mobile. Its spectacular verandah includes allegorical figures of the four seasons, arabesques, hearts, and intricately intertwined tendrils. Richards was a wealthy steamboat captain from Maine.

Opposite page: The Richards House verandah tastefully blends numerous motifs. Note the connected hearts on the railing in the foreground and the successful grouping of a vertical rinceau band, the allegorical figure, and an arabesque panel on the porch itself.

Left: Detail, winter, Richards House. Human figures in ornamental ironwork are rare.

Left: The old City Hall (1856) at 111 S. Royal Street displays intricate iron lunettes of woven wire held by cast floral clasps. The building presently serves as the Museum of Mobile, which has adopted this design element for its logo.

Right: Mobile's first cast iron facade adorned the 1860 Elgin Building, pictured here in an 1884 city directory advertisement for a later business.

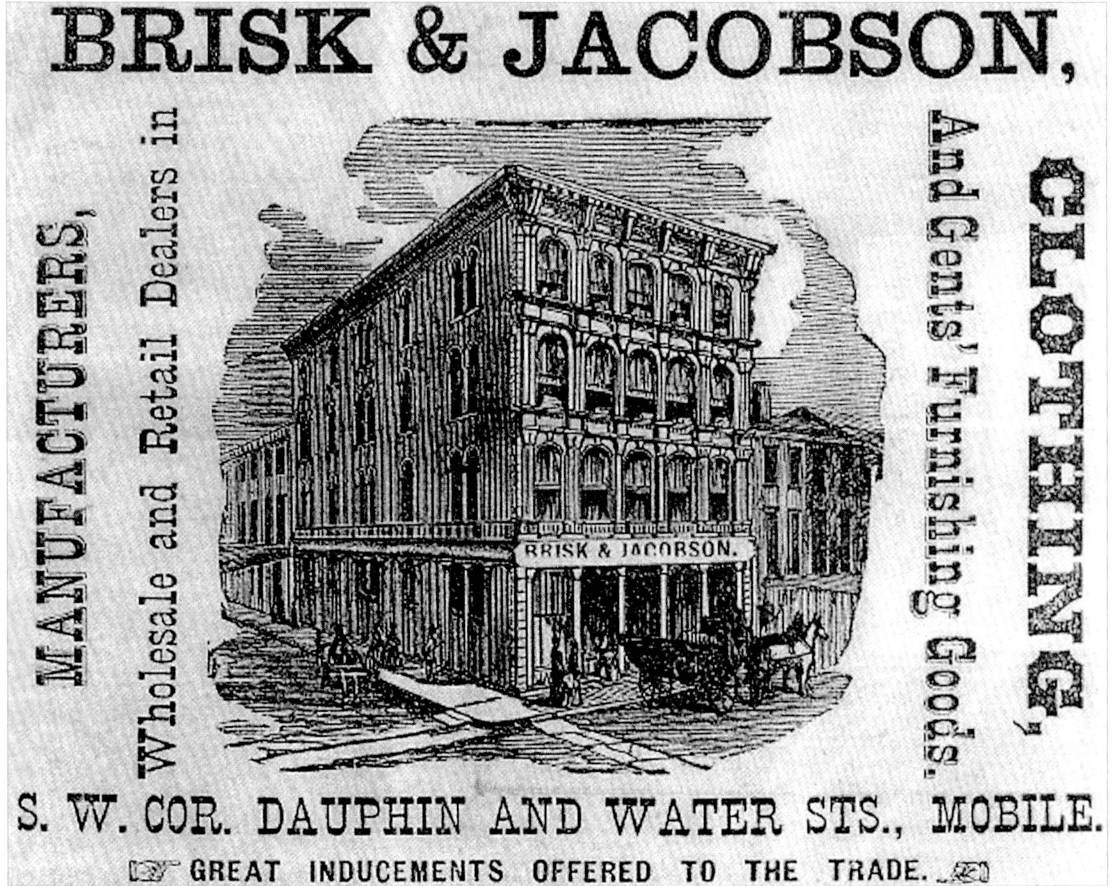

working through a local agent, and it arrived aboard a sailing ship in large sections. Designed by the firm's architect, J. H. Giles, the Daniels, Elgin facade is a four-story neo-Venetian wonder with large arched windows divided by paired Corinthian columns and capped off by a bracketed and denticulated cornice. In one of its later catalogs, Badger and Co. bragged, "all the large cities and towns have their fronts built of iron, ornamented in the most elaborate and varied styles of architecture."[35]

Detail, Elgin Building. Other than minor nicks and a little rust along a few seams, the cast iron elements of this facade have held up remarkably well.

By any measure, the ornamental ironwork trade in antebellum Mobile was a highly competitive but lucrative business. Local blacksmiths and foundries found it a worthwhile supplement to their larger industrial and agricultural orders, and agents like Alderson, Ellison, and Rouse were directly responsible for importing tons of decorative work from the large northern foundries. In fact, by 1860, Mobile was second only to New Orleans in the quantity of ornamental ironwork ordered from Wood's Philadelphia foundry. Not surprisingly, the Civil War strangled the trade. Wood's last shipment to Ellison was March 29, 1861, two weeks before Fort Sumter's bombardment.[36]

As Mobile's citizens turned their attentions to the war, their exotic little city presented a breathtaking exhibit of ornamental ironwork—from city hall's grilles and the sophisticated arabesques at the Richards House to the multitiered verandahs lining Dauphin Street and the massive fences surrounding Bienville Square and the cathedral. The hideous conflict would demonstrate cast iron's more sinister applications, but when the shooting stopped, Mobilians' love for its lacy, benevolent display returned unabated.

Chapter Two

Postwar Trade

Brokers, Mongers, Builders

Opposite page: Grape clusters adorn the back of this bench, cast by August Kling's Home Industry Foundry. Kling's operation was one of the most successful foundries in late-nineteenth-century Mobile.

WITH THE ONSET OF HOSTILITIES, MOBILE'S blacksmiths and foundries turned to full-time war production. Sword and knife blades were hammered out on anvils, cannon barrels and round shot cast, and ships fitted with light armor. By far the most innovative project took place at the Parks and Lyons machine shops, where the submarine *Hunley* was crafted from an old cast iron boiler. But with the armies siphoning off all eligible manpower and the blockade clamping down on imports, such efforts became more difficult to sustain. Surprisingly, given the dearth of raw materials, there is no evidence that Confederate authorities attempted to scrap the Port City's ornamental ironwork.

This was fortunate for aesthetic reasons but also practical ones. Iron fences helped protect property from errant pack animals and soldiers and camp followers that crowded into town, and balconies proved to be popular for watching military parades. On one such occasion, 2,200 Confederate troops led by Major General Braxton Bragg formed a column along Government Street, stretching from Royal Street out to Barton Academy. As it threaded its way through downtown, Bragg cantered alongside, and, according to a press account, excited ladies crowded balconies along the route and "waved their handkerchiefs."[1]

The Goldsmith House (1862) at 339 Church Street was completed just before the Civil War stifled residential construction. Like several other local high-style Italianate homes, this one features a carefully laid marble tile deck. An iron lamppost stands in the right foreground. Today this home, along with its twin next door, serves as an inn.

Balconies were also perfect for delivering speeches, and on October 24, 1863, President Jefferson Davis addressed Mobilians from the Battle House verandah. "He spoke with remarkably clear enunciation," the *Mobile Daily Register* reported, "his words penetrating far through the street, and were distinctly heard by most of the vast crowd gathered."[2]

James Henry Hutchisson, architect. (Courtesy C. L. Hutchisson Collection, University of South Alabama Archives.)

The war was difficult for everyone in the Port City, but a few individuals demonstrated superior abilities in meeting its challenges. Among these were two men, James Hutchisson and Daniel Geary, who were to become rivals in Mobile's postwar ornamental ironwork trade. Both were brave soldiers, capable leaders, and talented administrators. Their wartime experiences tempered them and made each a formidable adversary.

James H. Hutchisson was a young architect who had just established himself in private practice when the war came. He left a wife and two children when he enlisted in the Alabama Light Artillery. Enrolled as a sergeant, Hutchisson saw bloody action at Shiloh, where he was "remarkably self possessed," as one of his men recalled. After his transfer back to Mobile, his architectural knowledge was put to use at forts Morgan and Gaines, and by the winter of 1863 he had been promoted to captain. When Mobile fell a little more than two years later, Hutchisson and his men fled upriver in a desperate bid to escape capture, but they were cornered at Demopolis and taken. After his parole, Hutchisson returned to his little family with no resources but his wits to make ends meet.[3]

Daniel Geary, a fifty-year-old Irish immigrant, was a bookkeeper in the spring of 1861, with a wife and teenage stepdaughter, a modest house on Springhill Avenue, and one slave.[4] Upon enlisting as a lieutenant he was appointed ordinance officer for the city's defenses. His commanding officer outlined his duties in a long letter: "You are responsible not only for the instruction of officers and men in the mere drill at the guns," the officer wrote, "but for their thorough and minute instructions in the cutting of fuses, filling shell, elevations, ranges, the care of ammunition and everything that relates to the efficient service of the guns." In the winter of 1863, Geary applied for a promotion, which his commander enthusiastically endorsed: "His administrative qualities are of a fine order—and no better man could be selected to fill the vacant space."[5] When the city fell in the spring of 1865, Geary saw to it that all the guns under his supervision were spiked and the ammunition soaked, then he es-

Daniel Geary, iron broker. From Erwin Craighead, From Mobile's Past: Sketches of Memorable People and Events *(Mobile Printing Co., 1925).*

caped on foot. "Left my once happy home and family," he wrote in his diary, "crossed the bridge a refugee and a wanderer, leaving behind me a dear, dear wife, child, sister and two little nieces." A month later, a "sick and feverish" Geary was paroled at Meridian, Mississippi, and returned to his anxious family.[6]

Back in the Port City, Hutchisson and Geary found the old world entirely swept away. Freed slaves crowded the downtown, and Union troops bivouacked in Bienville Square. The economy was ruined, and local affairs were in federal hands. Though the city had been spared war's direct ravages, a terrific magazine explosion a month after Lee's surrender devastated a vast swath of downtown.

Neither man wasted much time lamenting his prospects amid this wreckage, however. Survival dictated work. Hutchisson hung out his shingle and solicited jobs, while Geary dabbled in real estate management. Neither of them likely was thinking about cast iron, but soon a troubling incident followed by a mysterious nocturnal heist reminded everyone of its existence.

Tensions were palpable over the 1865 July 4th holiday. A large gathering of freedmen in Bienville Square, under the watchful protection of black troops, elicited a sardonic article in the *Mobile Daily News*. "Quashie had his time yesterday," the paper sneered, "to his own liking, and with none to make him afraid." The *News* derided the "gaud" and "confidence" of the freedmen, made possible by "a detachment of their likes with loaded muskets and glittering bayonets to prevent the 'impertinent white folks' from going 'between the wind and their nobility.'" Despite its obvious distaste over this exercise of free assembly, the paper had to admit that property damage was minimal: "One of the antlers of the stag that adorned the mound was broken off, and other little mischiefs done, but that was about the worst of it."[7]

In this agitated racial climate, the cast iron slave boy inexplicably disappeared. On July 13, the *Mobile Daily News* detailed the perplexing occurrence under the headline, "Where Has He Gone?" In a slightly bemused tone the paper reported, "The 'American citizen of African descent,' that has flourished on the mound of the public square has mysteriously departed. He carried a lofty head and assumed a proud and imposing attitude while he guarded the denizen of the forest, and his absence is much deplored." Local speculation ran rampant: Had boisterous freedmen made off with Sambo? Or had assertive black troops, angered by this symbol of servitude, hurled him into the river? The real answer was several years in coming. In the meantime, a legend grew, and the stag, forlornly missing an antler, held solitary vigil on the mound.[8]

Only weeks later, the indefatigable agent Thomas Ellison died, leaving a widow and an estate worth $2,000. Among his assets were a few unsold iron pieces, including a hat rack, a table, and two gates. His indebtedness included $337 owed to Wood and Perot, and $100 to the blacksmith William Rouse for some repair and installation work. Though the agency had hardly made Ellison rich, it had provided a modest living and his widow some security at a time when many were not so fortunate. In the South's constricted postwar circumstances, the Robert Wood agency was a rare and promising opportunity.[9]

It was Daniel Geary who next secured it, by unknown means, but most likely through his earlier acquaintance with Ellison. In January 1866, Geary wrote to Robert Wood in Philadelphia asking to be his representative. He informed Wood that he had lived in the port city for thirty-one years and knew the town and its people intimately. He promised to be a diligent factotum and "send you a great many orders." Within a few weeks, Wood gave him the nod.[10]

DAN. GEARY, AGENT.

OFFICE:

Citizens' Savings Bank, cor. Water and Exchange Sts.,

MOBILE, ALA.

Garden and Cemetery Adornments

AT REDUCED PRICES.

☞ *Fountains, Vases, Verandahs, Summer Houses, Arbors, Chairs, Settees, Iron Furniture of every description; Patent Wire Work, Railings, Store Fronts, Door and Window Guards, Farm Fencing, etc., Bronze Work; Iron Stairs, spiral and straight, in every style of pattern; new and improved variety of Stable Fixtures—Hay Racks, Mangers, Stall Divisions, etc. Iron Railing for enclosing Cemetery Lots, Offices, Dwellings, Public Squares, etc., etc.*

Having fitted up our Foundry with special reference to the above class of work, we are now prepared to fill, with promptness, all orders for Bronze Castings, of every description, to which the subscribers would most respectfully call the attention of the public, as also to their varied and extensive assortment of Ornamental Iron Goods, the largest to be found in the U. S.

Daniel Geary advertisement from Farrow's Mobile City Directory, *1869.*

Geary's agency and the local iron trade can be followed in fascinating detail thanks to the survival of his complete business correspondence from 1866–78. Geary kept carbon copies of his letters to Wood, eventually binding them into two large volumes, which were saved by his step-grandson, Francois Diard, and donated to the Historic Mobile Preservation Society. Unfortunately, only a few of Wood's replies to Geary were preserved. Even so, the Diard Ironwork Ledgers open an arcane world in all its quotidian richness and, an especial boon to local history buffs, make possible the identification of dozens of unmarked iron pieces.

On February 12, 1866, Geary profusely thanked Wood for awarding him the agency. He pledged "strict attention to business" and asked for a catalog, price lists, and a "suitable cut for an advertisement in the papers." After setting up an office in the Citizen's Savings Bank at the corner of Water and Exchange streets, he called on Mrs. Ellison in an effort to settle her late husband's debt to Wood. She was cordial but none too helpful. Geary informed Wood that the widow was "not willing to make any acknowledgements of you against the estate," but she did give Geary the unsold ironwork and a couple of "very much defaced" design books. Geary wrote that he would attempt to sell the gates "to the best advantage."[11]

As he established himself, Geary badgered Wood for designs and price lists. These were the lifeblood of his business, and the greater the variety and the more up-to-date the designs, the more competitive he could be. On March 29 he complained, "I am very deficient in designs in both verandahs and railings" and "I am much needing designs of all kinds and prices." Two weeks later he wrote, "Send me specific prices for all kinds of castings vis door and window cils and caps. Collums. And plain and ornamental. Also, the Book of prices specifying the prices of posts etc. from the list just Rec'd I cannot tell when posts are included." Exasperated at not getting the literature he needed, Geary complained on April 21, "I am much annoyed for want of designs and etc. I am so limited in these articles it puts me back very much." Though Wood's replies are no longer extant, he apparently attempted to cultivate his new agent and find common ground, as indicated in a letter Geary wrote on April 16: "In reference to your remarks about peace I can only say with you amen. I thank God from my heart for it."[12]

Philadelphia Ornamental Iron Works.

ROBERT WOOD & CO.,
No. 1136 Ridge Avenue,
ROBERT WOOD. PHILADELPHIA, PA. THOS. S. ROOT.

Manufacturers of

Fountains, Vases, Statuary,

VERANDAHS, SUMMER HOUSES,
ARBORS, CHAIRS, SETTEES, &c., &c.,

Cast and Wrought Iron Railings,

For Public Buildings and Squares, Cemetery Lots, Garden Fences, Balconies, Roof Crestings, etc., in great variety of Patterns.

IRON STAIRS,

Spiral and Straight, of various Patterns and Styles. Special attention given this class of work.

LAMP POSTS,

For Fronts of Public Buildings, Hotels and City Streets, of Plain and Elaborate Designs.

STABLE FITTINGS,

Of Cast and Wrought Iron of New Improved Styles, such as Hay Racks, Stall Divisions, Mangers, Harness Brackets, Gutters, Traps, Ventilators, &c., &c.

WIRE WORK,

Of every Description. Wire Guards of Crimped Wire, Galvanized or Painted, in Plain or Ornamental Patterns.

GATES,

For Entrance to Cemetertes, Public Squares and Gentlemen's Country Seats, of Gas Tubing or Wrought Iron, both Single and Double, in elaborate and simple designs.

Estimates and Designs sent on application, stating the class of work desired.

Purchasers may rely on having all articles carefully boxed and shipped to the place of destination.

Above: A page from Robert Wood's 1868 catalog found tucked in Geary's correspondence indicates the range of ironwork available to the Mobile agent. (Courtesy Historic Mobile Preservation Society.)

Opposite page: The Horst House (1867) at 407 Conti Street includes ironwork ordered from Robert Wood and Co. While the verandah and fence are cast iron, the gate itself is wrought with some cast clasps. The address appears in the narrow brass plate above the star.

When a customer selected a design, Geary placed the order by mail (or sometimes telegraph) and handled the shipping and insurance. His agent's fee was the standard 10 percent that Ellison had received. With most verandahs priced around $1,500, this was a not inconsiderable cut in an era when laborers made only dollars a day. Most of the iron was shipped by sea, cushioned by sawdust in heavy wooden crates. When it arrived, Geary had it delivered to the job site, where it was erected by a mechanic, usually a local ironworker looking to make extra cash.[13]

Elegant stone curbing and dark pavers were generally purchased, boxed, and shipped along with fences and verandahs, and were not, as local legend asserts, salvaged from reeking ballast. Multicolored marble tiles were especially popular, laid in

AT LAW
407

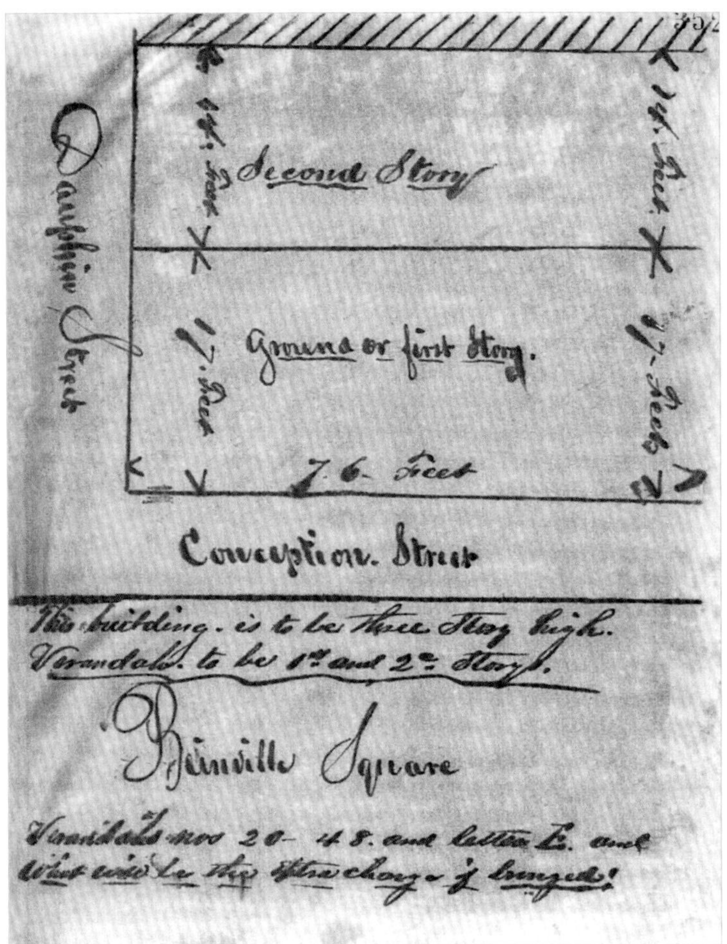

Above: Geary included this rough sketch in a letter to Wood asking for an estimate on a two-story balcony downtown. The diagonal lines across the top indicate the balcony's roof. (Courtesy Historic Mobile Preservation Society.)

Opposite page: The McCoy House (1873) verandah features mixed elements. The columns and heavy Gothic brackets are from Robert Wood and Co., while the railing with its anthemions is from an unknown supplier. Wood's catalog suggested a different railing, but for some reason the owner preferred this one.

diagonal patterns on Italianate-style porches like those of the Richards and Goldsmith houses. First a mason carefully set the stone and tile, then the mechanic pieced together the ironwork. Columns, railings, gates, and supports were leaded into neat mortises in the stone or brick, while drop friezes, brackets, and pendants were all bolted together to create the desired patterns.[14]

Unfortunately, there were headaches aplenty, and Geary had to troubleshoot at every stage of the process. To begin with, shipping by sail was frequently delayed by the vagaries of wind and weather, and on at least one occasion a local quarantine held up a brig in the lower bay. When an order arrived at the wharf, Geary anxiously prised open the crates, far too frequently finding that everything was not as it should have been. He was plagued by incorrect orders and pieces that didn't fit together properly or that had been broken by a particularly rough sea voyage. These issues had to be resolved through correspondence and time-consuming returns. Wood was invariably cooperative, but Geary and the purchaser often chafed at the delays.[15]

There were other problems as well, none more delicate than the issue of unpaid bills. When buyers were tardy with payments, Geary was forced to dun them while fending off Wood's inquiries. He proved to be adroit at the game, remaining attentive to business while managing to maintain the goodwill of both his customers and the foundry. One customer, commission merchant Price Williams, was so pleased with the fence he bought through Geary that he praised him as "a capital agent" and, whatever the irritants of the moment, Wood always took a reasonable position. Geary certainly found the business overall worthwhile, writing to his friend A. J. Mullaney that it was so good he "would not Swap [it] for any . . . in this Vilage."[16]

By far the most persistent, nagging problem was the competition. Geary did everything he could to maximize his advantages, including securing agencies with a foundry that dealt in heavier castings than Wood and with several marble yards that sold funerary pieces. With local foundries attempting to drum up business and architects and builders representing other out-of-town firms, things sometimes got nasty. The most unpleasant episode for Geary occurred in the summer of 1866, when James Hutchisson darkened his door.

Column detail, Chamberlain Building (1865), 551 Dauphin Street. Cast iron columns were frequently used on nineteenth-century storefronts. This one's floral capital is muddied by thick layers of paint. Note the delicately fashioned lunette at right.

Hutchisson maintained an office nearby on Conti Street. In one of his advertisements, he listed his services, including "Plans drawn, Specifications Written, Bills of Material made out, and everything in the line got up with neatness and dispatch."[17] Like Geary, he was having to scramble for work, and his drive and determination were paying off. In May he designed a three-story brick commercial building on Government Street and shortly thereafter got the contract to put up a large building for Messrs. Forcheimer, wholesale grocers. Hutchisson sensed a great opportunity in providing the structural cast iron that jobs like these required and the ornamental balconies and other appurtenances that more owners wanted. If Geary's version of events is to be credited, the methods Hutchisson employed to capitalize on these opportunities were at the very least unethical, if not despicable.[18]

GET YOUR IRON WORK AT HOME.

PHOENIX FOUNDRY

W. ROUSE, PROPRIETOR,

MANUFACTURER OF

IRON RAILING, VERANDAHS,

IRON FRONTS,

AND EVERY DESCRIPTION OF ORNAMENTAL IRON WORK.

IRON DOORS, SHUTTERS, BANK VAULTS, LOCKS, ETC.

☞ Can furnish any of the above named work at lower prices than they can be brought from any part of the North; and as to quality of work, I think mine will compare favorably with any brought here.

☞ Particular attention paid to Fencing Cemetery Lots. Call at

ROYAL, NORTH-EAST CORNER THEATRE ST.,

And see my Patterns, of which I have as large a selection as any Shop in the Union.

☞ For Sample of Work, see Battle House Verandah. ☜

Phoenix Foundry ad from Mobile City Directory, *1871. The owner, William Rouse, referred potential customers to a sample of his work at the Battle House Hotel.*

Sometime early in June, Hutchisson called on Geary at his office. As longtime residents of Mobile who had both participated in the defense of their city, the two men probably knew one another. No doubt they chatted about the war, grumbled about the occupation and the economy, and inquired after spouses and children. Hutchisson told Geary that he had a commission to build a fine brick house for which the owner wanted a verandah. He asked if he could look over some designs and make a tracing of the most likely one, with the understanding that if the owner fancied it, Geary would have the order. Together they opened the catalog, and Hutchisson flipped through its pages before settling on Verandah No. 23. With sure pencil strokes he traced the design, pocketed it, thanked Geary, and went out the door.[19]

To Geary's shock, Hutchisson promptly cut him out of the deal entirely by taking the drawing to local foundry owner (and former blacksmith) William Rouse, who cast the pattern in his shop. Aghast, ashamed of his naïveté, Geary wrote to Wood, "No honest man would stoop to anything so low."[20]

The Bernstein House (1872) at 355 Government Street features an iron verandah procured by Hutchisson. The Gothic Revival fence was salvaged from another property during the 1970s.

The incident made Geary hyperaware of his competition, and he became security obsessed. He informed Wood that he had posted a sign in his office forbidding the loan or tracing of patterns. He was now convinced that Hutchisson and local foundries would "do all in their power" to pirate designs. On June 27, he wrote to H. C. Oram, a Pennsylvania founder for whom he was also an agent, and cautioned, "Be careful your designs do not get into hands that could use them in foundries here." On August 29, Geary warned Wood: "There is a man named Kelly visiting your city. I understand [he is] well acquainted with your house his object in calling on you is to obtain your designs for Mr. Hutchisson and Mr. Rouse." Months later, a still-simmering Geary further cautioned Wood about Hutchisson, who was then traveling north: "Mr. Hutchisson a Sort of would be architect visits your city and New York for the purpose of getting an agency from the house of Spear and Jackson, New York. I have no doubt he will try and obtain one of your lists of prices. I think I will make him sick of it before he is done. Keep a look out for him, he is of medium size hair inclined to be red."[21]

Unfortunately, neither Geary nor Wood had any legal recourse, and the underhanded ploy that so outraged Geary's sense of honor apparently didn't trouble anyone else. Local businessmen and homeowners seemed only interested in getting ironwork at the cheapest possible price. If Geary had not already appreciated this fact, he surely did by January 1867, when he was the victim of yet more skullduggery.

After five three-story brick buildings burned that month, the owners announced plans to rebuild them with balconies. Both Geary and Hutchisson bid on the ironwork, and Geary had the low price. But to his astonishment, Hutchisson went behind his back to the owners and undercut his bid. Though Geary tried to counter, the owners went with Hutchisson. Geary complained to Oram that Hutchisson "acted . . . very dishonourably" but took some comfort in the fact that "all Master Mechanicks here think it a Very Singular proceeding" and reiterating, "I will make him sick of this transaction." But the reality was that Geary was going to have to be a lot quicker on his feet, and Wood willing to drive his prices down hard, if the agency was to prosper.[22]

Geary was anything but incompetent, however, and despite losing certain bids managed to win others. Among these was a lucrative order for fifty-eight iron benches for Bienville Square. On June 1, 1866, Geary informed Wood of the city's intention to purchase eight sixteen-foot benches and fifty eight-foot settees for the square. The sixteen-foot benches were to be curved for placement around the central mound. A New Orleans foundry "making hard for the Mobile trade" wanted the job, Geary wrote, but he was confident he could prevail, explaining, "The mayor and Both Boards are Strong friends of mine and if I can deliver this order in Mobile for less than the New Orleans establishment I will before long have another order." In conclusion, he emphasized that the benches be all iron, as "we have a class of loungers here who have a great propensity for using their pocket knives."[23]

A young boy poses on a Bienville Square bench, ca. 1895. Robert Wood's mark is visible just to the left of him. Cast iron amenities proved a great advantage in public spaces where rough usage prevailed. (Author's collection.)

Wood sent Geary a quote of $2,615, to which the agent added $160 for "freight, wharfage and drayage" before presenting it to the city.[24] John Hurtel, chairman of the Committee on Public Grounds, recommended that Geary's bid be accepted, "provided He puts them up at such points as may [be] designated without any further cost."[25] An elated Geary thanked Wood and speculated that the city might want more settees for Washington Square.[26]

Geary worked hard to maximize his opportunities, and he began to do steady business. He wrote to Oram asking a number of technical questions about cast iron facades, asserting, "I am anxious to have the fronts introduced."[27] He also did a little trade upstate when the former Confederate general E. W. Pettus of Selma ordered a cemetery fence. Throughout the late 1860s, as Mobile slowly recovered from the devastations of the war, Geary successfully brokered numerous sales, including railings and gates for James Elder in August 1866, a verandah for the Louis Durand buildings the following year, a swan fountain for a Government Street mansion in May 1868, and window guards for the Creole Fire Station when it was completed in 1869.[28]

The gazebo (1870) at the Convent of the Visitation, 2300 Springhill Avenue. At $380 it was not unreasonably priced, but the nuns had difficulty paying for it during Reconstruction.

Geary was a conscientious agent, and he broke an almost three-year silence in a brief postscript to Wood in May 1868: "Sambo the original that Stood for years in Bienville Square Mobile you no doubt recollect his mysterious disappearance on the Eve of July 4/65 he is in my possession as your property. Other parties claim him please inform me if you have Ever been paid for the darkey."[29] Years later, in an interview with *Mobile Register* editor Erwin Craighead, Geary elaborated on the incident. Given the large freedmen gatherings downtown, he had feared Sambo "might be injured," so one night he and a servant slipped into the square, concealed the three-hundred-pound figure in a croker sack, and hauled it away.[30]

Since Wood never expressed any desire to have the statue returned, Geary kept it hidden on his property until 1890, when he gave it to a local Catholic school. In the 1950s, Sambo moved again, this time to the front lawn of Oakleigh, an antebellum house museum that serves as the Historic Mobile Preservation Society headquarters. In 2001, still a political hot potato, he was loaned to Mobile's National African American Archives on Martin Luther King Jr. Avenue, where, sadly contemplative as ever, he stands today.

During the 1870s, the economy deteriorated, and Geary struggled to keep his business afloat. He repeatedly lamented political and financial conditions in his correspondence with Wood. On October 23, 1872, he wrote, "Nothing talked of but politics, cotton and dul times." A year later, it was the same: "As for Mobile, the prospects are bad. Very little doing in the way of building." By the summer of 1874, "Everyone complaining of hard times, and at least two thirds of the community idle."[31] Travelers' accounts confirm Geary's statements. Northern journalist Edward King passed through Mobile in 1874 and reported that it was "tranquil and free from commercial bustle."[32]

Frustrated by the torpor, Geary groused to Wood on September 15, 1870: "I have tried frequently to sell some of the lamp posts to our Hotels. The fact is they are controlled by a passel of Old fogies that have no Enterprise or ideas of modern improvement." Even when he did make a sale, matters sometimes got complicated. At the same time he was ineffectually pushing lampposts, Geary was approached by the Visitation Convent's Reverend Mother. She wanted a "useful as well as ornamental" gazebo to cover a well and a seven-foot bronze statue of Jesus to be "guilded with gold all over from head to foot." The statue was rejected as prohibitively expensive, but the Reverend Mother decided to order the gazebo for $380, provided Geary would allow her six months, interest free, to pay for it. Geary accepted the terms and obtained Wood's go-ahead. The gazebo was delivered just before Christmas, 1870, but to Geary's consternation, the foundry billed the convent before the agreed-upon six months had expired. "This gentlemen is not their agreement with me: nor mine with you," he huffed. "It places me in a Very unpleasant position." After a brief flurry of correspondence, Wood apologized for the misunderstanding and promised to abide by the original agreement. Geary traveled out Springhill Avenue to the convent to reassure the flustered sisters. The nuns were mollified, and Geary wrote that he expected more orders from them.[33]

Top and above: Details, gazebo at the Convent of the Visitation.

The Battle House Hotel, viewed from Royal Street. The highly decorative two-story verandah wrapped around the far side and continued on for 175 feet. From Artwork of Mobile and Vicinity *(Chicago: W. H. Parish Publishing, 1894).*

Bidding continued to be fiercely competitive, and Geary lost two important jobs in 1870. The first was a big ironwork order for a three-story building at Spring Hill College. Wood quoted Geary $2,866, more than $300 over the next highest bid. Geary responded, "I cannot understand how they do the work for So much less than you offer to do it." As he studied the numbers, Geary despaired over the figures for freight, insurance, and transport six miles out to the campus, all of which would have driven his price even higher.[34]

The second contract was for a new Battle House verandah. The hotel's old balcony had proven so popular that the owners decided to replace it in the spring of 1870 with a much larger and fancier version. Eager to land the job, Geary forwarded the specifications to Philadelphia and asked for an estimate. The proposed balcony was to be roofed, 158 feet long and 10 feet wide along the Royal Street elevation and

175 feet long and 7.5 feet wide along St. Francis Street, with 18-foot first-floor columns and 15-foot second-floor columns. Geary believed he had several factors in his favor. To begin with, Wood had supplied the original balcony when Ellison was his agent. Secondly, Geary was friends with the hotel's proprietor and declared the man was "very favorable to me and desirous I should get the contract." Unfortunately for Geary, Wood again supplied a figure, $6,950, that was well above the other bids. "I failed in Obtaining the Contract," Geary reported in a dispirited letter dated July 27. "There were five different estimates and from all I can learn the Committee acted very unfair in the matter. However, I have no fault to find as Some of them were So much lower than what I could put it up for that there was no chance for me." The winner was his nemesis William Rouse, whose "very massive" design came in at

Balcony detail on the south building (1885), Convent of the Visitation, J. H. Hutchisson, architect. Ornamental ironwork declined in popularity as the nineteenth century drew to a close, but competition among architects and foundries to supply it remained strong.

This fence post in Magnolia Cemetery was cast by Mobile's Gulf City Foundry, which flourished from 1870 to 1886. Foundries rarely marked their ironwork, making later identification difficult.

$2,100. Geary couldn't fathom how Rouse did it. "Seemingly he is working for the honor and glory of the thing," he wrote.[35]

As the decade advanced, Geary's troubles multiplied. A year after losing the Battle House contract, he seriously injured his back in a fall, and for months he was bedridden and unable to pay his bills. "The times here and all over the South are in a bad fix," he railed in a letter to his friend Mullaney. "Business paralised, the people afraid to Say there souls are there own, the whole country ruled by a pack of thieving officials holding their positions by fraud, negro rule and bayonets." To Wood he adopted a softer tone, thanking the founder for his leniency and understanding, expressing regret at Mobile's lack of building activity, and reporting that the competition remained "intense." By 1878 Geary's once busy agency had ground to a standstill. "My health has been bad for a long time," he wrote to Wood. "I have been idle So long I have lost heart to Stir around or to do anything. My health has been bad for one year, and for the past four years I have not earned five hundred dollars." Their long relationship, which so strongly impacted the city's physical appearance, came to an end.[36]

Mary and August Kling confidently pose in this ca. 1880 photograph. (Courtesy Mary Francis Alexander.)

During the remaining twelve years of his life, Geary relied on bookkeeping and real estate management for a modest living. When he died in May 1892, three months after his wife, he was $2,000 in debt, which his attorney settled by selling his Springhill Avenue house. His obituary in the *Mobile Daily Register* lauded him as one of "Mobile's oldest and most respected citizens," listed his memberships in a Mardi Gras society and a volunteer fire company, and noted his occupation as a bookkeeper. There was no mention of his association with Wood.[37]

Available records after 1878 do not indicate that anyone succeeded Geary as Wood's agent in Mobile. Too many other foundries, local and out of town, crowded the market. In 1880, just two years after Geary's last letter to Wood, Mobile was home to five large foundries and numerous small-time artisans. The iron industry was one of the most robust enterprises in town, behind gristmills and lumber. Just as in the antebellum era, the ironworkers' bread and butter came from big jobs on steamships and locomotives, but all of them solicited ornamental projects.[38]

The most successful of these postwar operations was the Home Industry Foundry, operated by a German immigrant named August Kling. In 1884, a booster publication highlighted the firm, which at that time employed fifty men. According to the profile, "None but skilled mechanics are engaged, and good wages are paid, thus insuring the best work possible in both manufacturing and repairing." The foundry's business extended into Mississippi and Florida, and its owners entertained "a fine prospect for further increase."[39]

Kling took a long time to reach such an exalted plateau. He was born in Buehl, Germany, in 1844 and served a mechanical apprenticeship there before coming to America in 1865. Shortly after his arrival in Mobile, he signed on with John Lang as a machinist-finisher. Lang's shop was a small one, but he was an accomplished craftsman with a flourishing trade. Kling would have thoroughly mastered his skills there and met most of the architects and builders then working.[40]

In 1871, Kling took two major steps. He married and went into business for himself. His bride, Mary Oberkirch, was also a German immigrant, and together the couple eventually had six children. Kling's first independent shop was located on Conti Street downtown, but shortly thereafter he moved it to the corner of State and Water streets, closer to the river.[41]

In the spring of 1884, the foundry was destroyed by fire. Undaunted, Kling hired James H. Hutchisson (who had a knack for befriending local founders) to build a new plant. Hutchisson was well acquainted with the iron making process and

Butt-Kling House, 254 N. Jackson Street. Built in 1857 for the architect Cary Butt with an iron porch, window guards, fence and gate, this house was purchased by August Kling and his wife in 1889. Though Kling's foundry produced ornamental work, he was happy to retain the original iron on his own home.

Left: Kling's Home Industry Foundry belches smoke in this detail from a company letterhead. (Courtesy Mary Alice Walsh Helms).

Below: Detail, Ehrgotte Kreb's 1891 "Bird's Eye View of Mobile" showing Kling's foundry and its relation to the all-important river. (Courtesy University of South Alabama Archives)

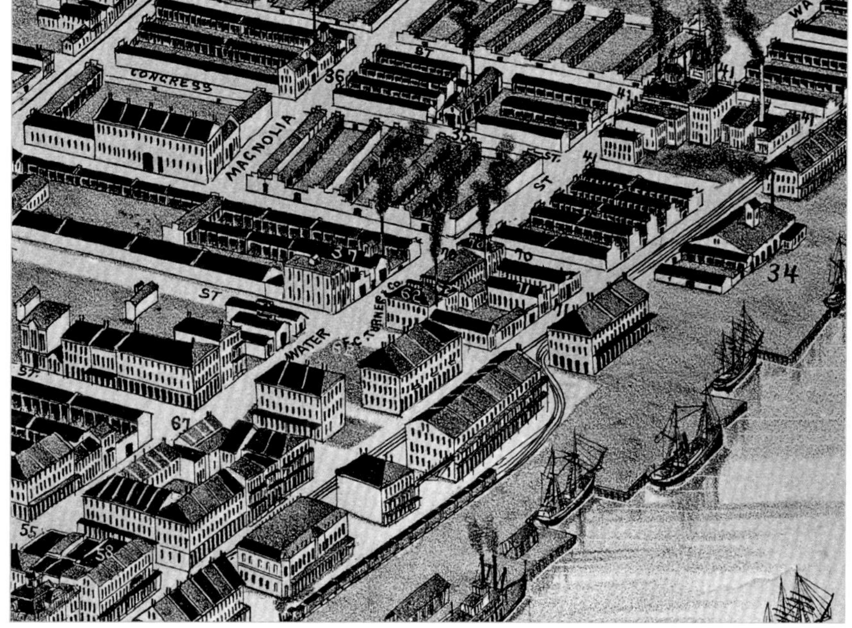

divided the structure into three parts—foundry, machine shop, and blacksmith shop. In an admiring account, the *Mobile Daily Register* especially enthused over the cupolas "of a melting capacity of five tons per hour" and the blacksmith shop's "eight-hundred weight Massey hammer of the best English make." The paper praised Kling's "high degree of executive and financial ability" in recovering from the fire so quickly.[42]

Unfortunately, bad luck struck again that November when a boiler exploded. The press reported the incident in a detailed story that forcefully illustrates the dangerous nature of foundry work. According to the article, "The shock was instantaneous, and blew the engine straight through to Water Street, a distance of 60 feet." The boiler "passed through the rear wall, broke the shafting, tore up the floor of the second story, destroying all the machinery in its path, and after tearing a hole in the street wall, from ground to roof, landed on the side walk in an inverted position." Incredibly, no one was seriously hurt, but the reporter interviewed several workers who described close calls. One of the black laborers, William Davis, who had been standing at a grindstone, related, "When the things commenced coming down so fast I thought the Judgement Day had come and the whole world was falling on me." Davis said he was covered by bricks and, after he clawed his way out, ordered his feet to "carry me away from dis place."[43]

Indomitable as ever, Kling repaired the damage, and the Home Industry Foundry resumed full production. Significant commissions included architectural iron for the Mobile Brewery, decorative cresting around the German Relief Hall's turret, the

Right: Gallery, Butt-Frazier House, 256 State Street. Kling's foundry supplied this ironwork for a new homeowner in 1897, more than forty years after the house itself was constructed. Its sinuous lines and grape clusters are well within the Victorian tradition, though the execution is more delicate than midcentury examples. This is one of the latest residential iron galleries in the city.

Opposite page: Late-nineteenth-century homeowners were enamored of floral motifs in their ornamental ironwork, as exhibited by these grape clusters on the Butt-Frazier gallery.

fine gallery on the Frazier House at 256 State Street, and ironwork on the Monroe County Courthouse. "The concern has achieved the highest reputation," an 1895 business publication boasted, "its specialty being to turn out the best of work, made from selected raw material by highly skilled workmen under practical and experienced supervision. The house is in a position to supply many products which formerly could only be obtained in the North and West."[44]

Kling died in 1918 at the age of 74. The *Mobile Register* eulogized him as "one of the best known foundrymen on the Gulf Coast." His funeral was held at the cathedral, and the entire workforce of the Home Industry Foundry attended.[45] Three Kling sons carried the business forward until 1929, when it finally folded. In a 2003 interview, one of Kling's granddaughters, Mary Francis Alexander (b. 1913) de-

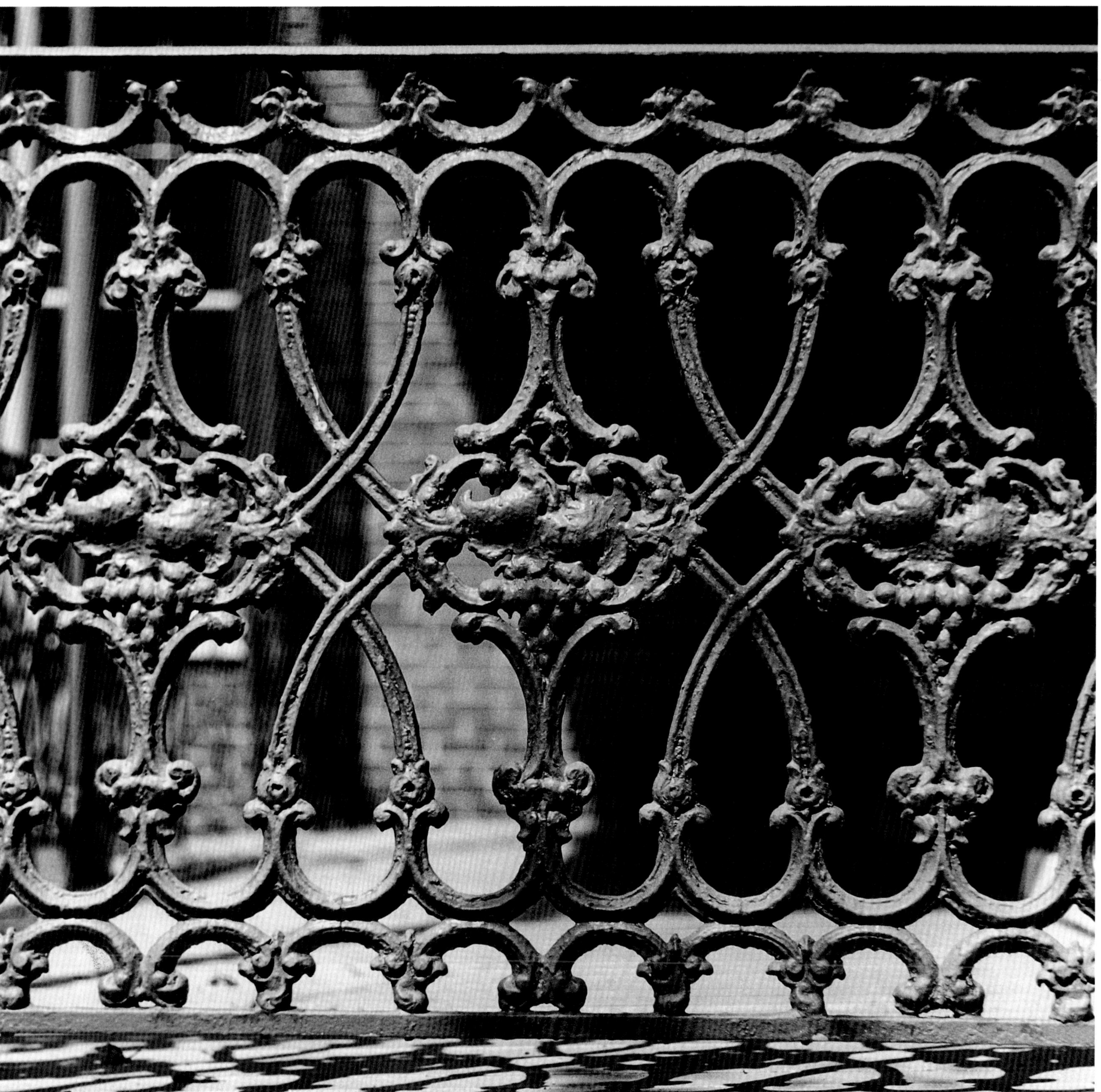

scribed a childhood visit to the foundry. "It was a big, big place," she recalled. "Seemed to take up the whole block. I remember the machinery, steps up to the pattern shop and at the other end of the building the molding floor. That dirt was black as anything." Ornamental ironwork had largely passed out of vogue by the time Alexander visited, but she remembered elaborate designs on the walls and an ongoing demand for decorative iron benches.[46]

By the end of the nineteenth century, all of the hard work by men like Ellison, Geary, Hutchisson, Rouse, and Kling had borne glorious fruit. Downtown Mobile was literally cluttered with iron balconies, lampposts, fences, gates, benches, store-

Above: Home Industry Foundry benches such as this one were popular commodities well into the twentieth century.

Opposite page: Detail, gallery, Butt-Frazier House. As these slender contrasting balusters demonstrate, the Home Industry Foundry was fully capable of producing high-quality ornamental ironwork.

The Athelstan Club on Bienville Square, ca. 1879. The square's unpopular fence (of which there are few photographs) is visible at lower left, and a portion of another balcony protrudes at right. By the late nineteenth century ornamental ironwork was everywhere downtown. (Courtesy Historic Mobile Preservation Society.)

fronts, grates, and sundry other geegaws and contraptions. The profusion of sidewalk balcony supports presented an unusual dilemma for the electric company. In the fall of 1886, its president petitioned the city for permission to place power poles out in the street, because "on several squares in the business portion of the City the Galleries and awnings prevent the erection of poles on the sidewalk."[47] The problem was particularly acute on Dauphin, St. Francis, St. Joseph, Royal, Water, and Commerce streets.

As the electric company's experience indicates, Mobilians liked their ironwork and required that it be accommodated amid the hurly-burly of progress. But on at least one occasion, new ironwork replaced existing. In the spring of 1889, the city announced major renovations for Bienville Square. The unpopular massive fence that Ellison had supplied back in 1858 was sold for scrap, and plans were unveiled for new pathways and an attractive cast iron fountain to replace the deer in the square's center. City records do not indicate who supplied the large four-basin fountain, but its construction was followed with interest. On March 31, 1890, the *Mobile Daily Register* reported, "The fountain has arrived and is being put in Bienville Square." Two weeks later it updated readers, "The fountain is rearing its head in Bienville Square and looks to be fully 23 feet high. The old oak trees stand guard and add much majesty and beauty to the spot."[48] The deer so firmly in residents' affections was removed to Washington Square, where it remains to this day, more beloved than ever.

Washington Square, from a 1906 postcard. Iron benches sit empty while a child straddles the deer. (Courtesy University of South Alabama Archives.)

Opposite page: The Bienville Square fountain (1890) was dedicated to Dr. George A. Ketchum, president of the Bienville Water Works and an advocate of a pure water supply. Existing records do not indicate the fountain's origin, but the bottom basin exactly matches others fabricated by the J. L. Mott Ironworks, New York.

Right: Detail, bottom basin, Bienville Square fountain. Water gushes from satyrs flanked by floral spacers.

The fountain was one of the last important cast iron projects downtown. As the twentieth century progressed, changing tastes and more efficient materials like steel eclipsed ornamental ironwork. Even as it passed from favor, however, the port city's profusion of lacy iron began to attract outside notice and interest. Ironically, Mobilians themselves were becoming oblivious to it. The twentieth century brought wrenching change. A world war and urban development drastically altered the downtown, and tons of ornamental ironwork were lost or scrapped. Preservationists worked hard to save what they could and took pride that what survived embodied the city's very soul.

FOR SALE

Chapter Three

Legacy

Romance, Ruin, Renaissance

Opposite page: Detail, new gallery, Burke Building, 1 N. Royal Street (ca. 1880/1988). In recent years numerous downtown building owners have refurbished or added balconies, in some cases copying old patterns.

IN EARLY APRIL 1892, A MIDWESTERN JOURNALIST TRAVELED to Mobile and became the first outsider to publicly notice its ironwork. His article appeared in the Lyons, Kansas, *Tribune* and was reprinted for Mobile readers under the headline, "Graceful Description from a Kansas editor." The unnamed newspaperman's hosts showed him the local sights, including the Bay Shell Road, the oyster fleet, a dredge, and a lumber mill, but it was the city's distinctive architecture that entranced him. He commented on the prevalence of walls and courtyards that provided residents with calm sylvan retreats amid the urban bustle. "There are porches too," he marveled, "two stories in height and with latticed iron-work ornamentation, and many other things in architecture entirely novel to us."[1]

After the turn of the century such recognition, tinged with delight and romance, became commonplace even as the use of ornamental ironwork faded away. President Wilson was by far the most prominent individual to address the subject, but other people were intrigued as well. In 1925 Dr. Allen Albert, an Illinois resident, an officer in the Rotary International, and a self-described "city specialist," came to Mobile and instantly grasped the importance of its ironwork. "I am fascinated with your iron lace," he wrote to a resident. "It is a type of architectural decoration that is unique, a characteristic feature that should be emphasized in the future development of the city." This recognition was extraordinary and decades ahead of its time.[2]

Walker Evans's 1936 detail of the Ketchum House verandah, 400 Government Street. Like many other visitors to the Port City, Evans was captivated by its ironwork. This is his only known image of Mobile. (Courtesy Library of Congress.)

Nine years later, Carl Carmer, an Ivy League English professor guest teaching at the University of Alabama, penned an admiring description in his book *Stars Fell on Alabama*. "Mobile stays in the heart, loveliest of cities," he wrote. "Long low two-story buildings, their intricate iron balconies interrupted here and there by signs—'Sailors' Supplies,' 'The Army and Navy Store,' line the narrow streets. Sometimes the balcony overhangs the sidewalk and makes a roofed passage for pedestrians, ornate iron pillars supporting it at the street's edge." Like Dr. Albert, Carmer was enthralled by cast iron but less attuned to its potential economic benefit.[3]

As these passages clearly demonstrate, Mobile's ornamental ironwork had a great deal to do with visitors' reactions during the first half of the century. It was so obvious and so spectacular that the WPA guide to Alabama, published in 1941, repeatedly referenced it: "New business structures and old houses, with iron lace-work balconies still intact, stand side by side. In the shadow of a ten-story office building is a garden that might have been transplanted from Seville or from Cadiz and a fountain, almost hidden by adjacent structures, plays behind a beautiful wrought iron fence."[4] The guide highlighted numerous examples, including the Cathedral fence, City Hall's lunettes, Barton Academy's gates, and many verandahs. Photographs reinforced the belief that Mobile was more European than its upstate neighbors.

Detail, Cathedral gate. This ironwork was among that highlighted in the 1941 WPA guide to Alabama.

Boosters were pleased by all the positive press but failed to understand how things like old buildings and fancy ironwork could materially advance the city. Their energies were bent toward securing new railroad connections, enlarging the port, and attracting industry. Nor did everyday Mobilians, most of whom were not well traveled, readily fathom the potential of their too-familiar landmarks. Sadly, this ignorance was to be a recipe for disaster.

Elizabeth Fonde, a local civic worker and chamber of commerce member, was one of the earliest Azalea City residents to realize the value of ornamental ironwork and to fear for its future. In a magazine article written in 1929, she lamented the fact that many grand downtown residences had been converted into boardinghouses and their ironwork "gone to the junk dealers at a few cents per hundred pounds." She also described what would soon become a widespread practice among the city's first families—"the preservation of some of the beautiful iron work by removal to new homes." Fonde was not all doom and gloom, however, and acknowledged that some Mobilians "are awake to the possibilities."[5]

Foremost among these visionaries was Olive Brooks, a Port City native living in Gotham, who authored a long essay titled "Old Cast-Iron Work in Favor" for the September 8, 1929, *New York Times*. Brooks presented a thorough description of wrought and cast iron and their manifestations in her hometown. She demonstrated a solid aesthetic knowledge, recognizing that Mobile's ironwork was "inspired by the Gothic, Grecian and rococo revivals of the nineteenth century" rather than French or Spanish colonial antecedents. She also realized how the local context—"the soft quality of the light tones, and the background of luxuriant trees and shrubs"—contributed to its romantic allure. And like Fonde, she recognized the threats it faced. "For the owner of almost any tall house of ante-bellum days has more than once been called to her door by a gentleman desiring to purchase the front gate or the entire fence, and, failing in this, at least insisting on the purchase of the little side balcony." Brooks declared that most Mobilians would consider this "virtual family dishonor" but was compelled to admit that "tons of iron of beautiful workmanship were sold for scrap and carted away to the furnaces in an attempt to modernize Mobile before the worth of the old iron began to be appreciated."[6] Brooks's article alerted middle-class Mobilians to the treasures in their midst in no-nonsense, accessible prose. It was by far the most exposure the city's ornamental ironwork had received until then.

Book cover, Etchings of Old Mobile, *1938. Local colorists throughout the South liked to pair antiquities with rustic caricatures. (Courtesy MAM Arts and the Estate of Marian A. Macpherson.)*

Not to be outdone, the *Mobile Register* published its own story in 1932. Part history and part folklore, the anonymous article ran under the rhyming subhead, "Decorations of Another Time Are Precious Relics of This Clime Where French and Spanish Lines Commingle in Curious Old Designs." The article praised the "indescribably delicate and fragile" patterns displayed on local balconies and wondered how they had been "achieved in so cold and hard a medium." Several large photographs were included, set off by artistic borders.[7]

Fonde's and Brooks's articles and the *Register's* coverage left no doubt that Mobile's ironwork was becoming famous. Just as in New Orleans and Charleston, local colorists emerged to celebrate it in literature and art. The first of these was Marian Acker Macpherson, a former Mardi Gras queen and Junior League founder, who resided in the LeVert House on Government Street. After studying art in

New England, she returned to Mobile and established a little studio in the old doctor's office next door to her house. In 1932 she printed a collection of her etchings with accompanying captions titled *Prints of the Past from Old Mobile*. Her motivations were essentially antiquarian, as she stated in the introduction, "I have not attempted to relate or depict history in detail, but only to preserve and keep intact some bit of the rare charm and color of Old Mobile." She published an enlarged edition, *Etchings of Old Mobile*, in 1938 and eight years later a guidebook, *Glimpses of Old Mobile*, which remained in print as late as 1983. Macpherson loved the city's ironwork and included etchings of fences, gates, and balconies in her books, which enjoyed wide local circulation.[8]

The Bragg-Mitchell Mansion (1855) at 1906 Springhill Avenue features a small balcony that inspired a bit of rhetorical excess during the 1930s.

Mobile's ironwork was also extolled in *Historic Homes of Alabama and Their Traditions*, a 1935 book sponsored by the National League of Pen Women. In a description of the Bragg House, a bracketed Greek Revival mansion on Springhill Avenue, Mrs. Willie Hughes Tarpley enthused, "The iron work of the entrance and that of the romantic balcony above is in silver gray arabesque, like the delicate frost work of winter nights."[9] Where Mobile's ironwork was concerned, it seemed, flowery excess and syrupy allusion had become the rule. More serious research and evaluation were overdue.

The opportunity came when the federal government created the Historic American Buildings Survey in 1934 to provide work for architects and engineers. The Mobile Team, which included George B. Rogers, Nicholas Holmes, Sr., and Fred Clarke, established a separate category for ironwork, arbitrarily divided into early, middle, and late periods. Their documentation included measured drawings, black-and-white photographs, and historical data sheets, all of which went to the Library

The Sledge House (now demolished), 52 S. Jackson Street, recorded by HABS in 1937. Originally constructed in 1848 for a sail maker, this house had its ironwork added somewhat later, a not unusual circumstance as such ornament gained popularity. The rear galleries would have remained wood. Note the double carriage gates at left. (Courtesy HABS Collection, University of South Alabama Archives.)

of Congress. They tabulated hundreds of pieces, including fences in Magnolia Cemetery, residential verandahs, gates, hitching posts, and commercial storefronts along the river. Despite their methodical approach, the HABS people were not immune from ironwork's charm. In an article for the *Birmingham News-Age Herald*, the wife of Alabama's HABS coordinator, writing under the pen name Varian Feare, thrilled to the craftsmanship exhibited by City Hall's lunettes. "We look at the swell of their curves," she wrote, "the gentle turning of one section into another, the movement is as defined as that of ocean swells that rise and break, and know that the smithy who worked them had the eye and heart of an artist."[10]

A 1937 Life *magazine article featured this picture of railcars in Mobile captioned, "Japan Wolfs U.S. Scrap." Plenty of ornamental work ended up in such shipments. (Courtesy S. Blake McNeely Collection, University of South Alabama Archives.)*

As the HABS surveyors scrambled about town, measuring and recording ironwork, they knew it was endangered, foremost by scrap dealers but also by well-meaning owners who treated it like a portable amenity. In an unpublished monograph written around 1935, team member Frances Beverley was most irked by the latter trend. In her view, to take decorative iron off an antebellum home and "stick it on the front of a bungalow" was nothing less than "desecration."[11]

Yet it was the salvage dealers who were doing the most damage. Scrap iron had always had some value, of course—several companies bid to remove the Bienville Square fence in 1889—but during the 1930s Japan's Pacific rampage created a bull market that American junkmen rushed to supply. By 1935 so much of Mobile's old ironwork had been sold off that at least one frequent visitor noticed the change. The newspaper quoted the "much traveled tourist" as saying "the community is taking no measures to preserve the features which make Mobile so distinctive and of particular charm to visitors." The traveler was alarmed that numerous balconies had "fallen under the crowbars of wrecking crews."[12] E. B. Sledge, who was born in 1923 and grew up in Mobile, recalled Japanese ships "with the red meatball on their smokestacks" lined up in the river to receive this plunder.[13]

USO CLUB

Horrified by Japanese depredations in China, the U.S. Congress finally imposed a scrap ban in the fall of 1940. The *Mobile Register* ran a short article on the ban, under the subhead, "Nipponese big buyers of junk in U.S. cities."[14] Unfortunately, the reprieve was short lived. Once the United States entered the war just over a year later, its own scrap needs quickly became omnivorous.

In June 1942, war production chief Donald M. Nelson alerted Americans that salvage drives would likely "go well beyond what is normally considered scrap." He specifically referenced decorative ironwork that had been melted down in Europe, and concluded, "Any one of us can walk down any street in Washington and see substantial quantities of metals that might thus be used."[15] *Mobile Register* columnist Howard Barney vigorously protested the idea. "Take our men, money and machines, but spare Mobile's famous iron grillwork as long as possible," he pleaded. "Mobile will gladly surrender the most distinguishing feature of its early American period, if such action is needed to win the war; but let it be preserved as long as there are other sources upon which to draw." Barney made a direct link between the Port City's ironwork and its economic well-being when he declared, "It helps cash registers play a merry tune during the tourist seasons."[16]

Opposite page: The Knights of Columbus Building (originally the Battle-Ross House) at 602 Government Street served as the local USO headquarters during World War II. Unfortunately, not all of the Port City's ornamental ironwork fared so well during those years. This house was itself demolished in 1969 and its lace relocated to a Dog River property. (Courtesy S. Blake McNeely Collection, University of South Alabama Archives.)

World War II had a profound effect on Mobile. The city's population doubled with war workers, and every spare room was pressed into service and new housing constructed to accommodate them. Most of these people were poor whites from rural Georgia, Alabama, and Mississippi with no connections to the city's storied past. Yet crowded as it was with backcountry rustics living in tents and scantling board shacks, Mobile still retained a languid, graceful, Old South feel, thanks in part to its ironwork. The writer John Dos Passos passed through in 1943 and found a "mouldering old Gulf seaport" with an "ancient dusty elegance of tall shuttered windows under mansard roofs and iron lace overgrown with vines and scaling colonnades shaded by great trees."[17]

E. B. Sledge, serving overseas with the First Marine Division, had cause to remember his hometown's ironwork after a close call during the Battle of Peleliu. In a letter to his mother, one of the founders of the Historic Mobile Preservation Society, he found a little humorous irony in a Japanese mortar attack on his position: "I was standing up and saw the nearest shell out of the corner of my eye. I hit the ground just about when it did, the concussion was awful and my eyes caught a lot of powder and dust. One piece of shrapnel hit my leg but it was spent and didn't hurt.

Honestly when it was quiet again I thought to myself, 'That was probably Mobile old iron lace work about a year or so ago.'"[18]

Despite the junkmen's ravages, post–World War II Mobile still retained plenty of ironwork. Veterans like Sledge, returning home after two or three years away, once again saw the familiar balconies lining downtown streets. Bienville Square, with its grand oaks, plashing fountain, and battered old iron benches remained the community's centerpiece, and city officials conscientiously maintained it. In early 1947 new sod was laid, water lines installed, and the sidewalks widened. Officials also voted to spend $12,000 for new benches, to be locally cast by the Gulf Foundry division of the Waterman Steamship Corporation. Because of the deep public affection for the venerable originals, Wood's patterns were copied, thus preserving the square's nineteenth-century ambience.[19]

In the war's waning days, a former Junior League president and WPA advisory board member named Kathleen Yerger Johnstone wrote a short, inventive little appreciation of local ironwork. "Yes, I am a collector too," she announced, "but I can't display my treasures on glass shelves. I cannot even own my discoveries, for it would take an armory to house them. I must content myself with photographs, for I am a woman of iron."[20] In Johnstone's view, downtown was an alfresco museum, a smorgasbord of artifacts in plain sight. Unfortunately, losses continued apace, and greater tragedy was in the offing.

Opposite page: A Mobile belle relaxes on the verandah of the Richards House in 1946. Blake McNeely was among the first in a long line of local photographers to pose beautiful women with breathtaking ironwork in an effort to conjure the Old South. This image was not used in his book. (Courtesy S. Blake McNeely Collection, University of South Alabama Archives.)

In 1946 local printer and freelance photographer S. Blake McNeely published an outsized volume of his images that beautifully illustrated Johnstone's point. *Bits of Charm in Old Mobile* features dozens of black-and-white photographs of local architecture. Like Macpherson before him, McNeely was more interested in capturing "what is left of old landmarks and interesting sidelights" than in doing a comprehensive survey or serious research. His brief introduction includes language typical of local colorists: "Clusters of grapes, sheaves of grain, flowers, gods and goddesses, all were 'frozen' into intricate and fascinating patterns—'Iron Lace', Mobilians love to call it."[21] But it is the pictures that are significant, and they accurately portray downtown Mobile before urban renewal did its worst.

Mobile's ironwork continued to attract the attentions of homegrown artists and writers. Caldwell Delaney, a patrician local historian, and Clark S. Whistler, a talented pen and ink man, collaborated on *Remember Mobile*, an appealing popular history published in 1948. The book's cloth cover exhibits an anthemion arabesque motif, and many of Whistler's meticulous drawings illustrate iron fences, balconies, and the like. Delaney's prose is baroque but grounded in serious research. He was stirred by an abiding love for his city and its ironwork, "designed to finish a façade with elegance in perfect taste."[22] *Remember Mobile* is suffused with a slight melancholy, a sense that a more cultured past has slipped beyond reach.

The Bellingrath House, 1935, in south Mobile County displays decorative ironwork salvaged from the old Southern Hotel. Today, literally tons of relocated ironwork may be found throughout the bay area. (Courtesy Bellingrath Gardens Collection, University of South Alabama Archives.)

Two years later, the husband and wife team of William and Anne Shillito Howard published *Enchantment in Iron*, a mix of purple prose and meticulous sketches. Anne Howard was an amateur poet and, like most other writers confronting cast iron, could not resist imaginative flights. In one passage she conjured a mystical scene involving a naturalistic iron verandah at sunrise: "Acorns and leaves of alien oaks, long fixed in mortal stillness, will be lustered with bronze and emerald, and tremble with joyous whisperings. Nor will supporting trellises content themselves as base metals, but, touched by the moment of transformation, brackets and spirals and lattices will flash a golden salutation to the sun."[23] William Howard's drawings on the other hand are an exercise in verisimilitude. They include correct renditions of gates at the cathedral rectory on Government Street and the U.S. Marine Hospital on St. Anthony Street. Like other efforts by local colorists, *Enchantment in Iron* accurately depicts ironwork's appearance but is unable to provide any kind of realistic historic context. Its aim was essentially romantic. This was useful insofar as it developed local awareness.

Novelist and bon vivant Eugene Walter included an evocative description of cast iron in his 1953 Lippincott award-winning novel *The Untidy Pilgrim*. His narrator, a young man from upstate, approaches a decaying Mobile town house, "with high iron porches painted white, and a side wing hid in wisteria vines and crepe myrtle trees, dense and jungly." At the gate—"a lyre and fool's bauble twined with grapevines"—the protagonist reads the family name, "FIFIELD," before pushing it open on rusty hinges. "Going up the perforated iron steps I jumped, for when I stepped on the third step it was wobbly and clanged like a firebell when you stepped there." The narrator discovers the Port City to be a place apart, more mysterious and colorful than Birmingham. Walter deftly uses the antebellum brick house with its vine-choked, creaky cast iron to help convey this truth.[24]

This modern downtown hotel, constructed during the 1960s, employs underscaled reproduction ironwork in an attempt to capitalize on Mobile's distinctive sense of place. Government Plaza, built in 1996, looms in the background.

All of these writings and illustrations had their effect, and throughout the 1940s and 1950s there was considerable local interest in cast iron, which sometimes led to unfortunate results. As the suburbs grew and downtown declined, the pernicious practice of removing old ironwork and placing it on new houses increased. In some cases, people salvaged the iron from their family property; in others they purchased it from junk dealers. This was widely viewed as preservation rather than vandalism, an attitude mirrored by the *Mobile Register* in a 1948 article. "Where buildings have lived their age and have been torn down for progress," the article stated, "the iron work has not been sacrificed. It lives on in porches and balconies and fences of Mobile's newer homes, firmly rooted in new surroundings."[25]

Today relocated old Mobile ironwork may be found all over the bay area, and determining its original source has long been a preservationist's parlor game. Mary Jane "Iron" Inge, a tourist guide during the 1940s and presently a volunteer at the Museum of Mobile, explained in an interview that it is not difficult to identify fugitive remnants. "You can ride around and see ironwork and get out of your car and ring that doorbell and they can tell you right where it came from," she said.[26] Inge has compiled a long list of such pieces. A typical entry reads, "Point Clear, Mr. and Mrs. Peter Gaillard (Bernard Ladd) [property], Iron fence across front was at original Providence Hospital on St. Anthony Street near Marine Hospital and St. Joseph's Church. USA Archives has a picture. Notice the unusual catch on gate."[27] Other listings pinpoint the old Bienville Square gates, also in Point Clear, as well as a fountain from a Government Street mansion now on display outside a Fairhope social club. While it is fortunate that these pieces were saved at all, in their new settings they no longer excite. Torn from their historic context, they are mere whispers of a bygone age.

La Clede Hotel (1855), 150–60 Government Street. The restoration of this building and its large cast iron galleries during the early 1980s led other downtown property owners to restore or even add balconies.

Given the growing demand and limited access to historic ironwork, local foundries marketed new pieces, sometimes copied from the old patterns. General Metal Works, a small company on Virginia Street that operated from 1947 to 1957, printed a promotional brochure that trumpeted the "charm, hospitality and fine taste" of ornamental iron for the contemporary homeowner.[28] Among its illustrated patterns for porch rails were the alluringly named Plantation Grape, Admiral Semmes, French Quarter, Belle, and Creole designs. According to a 1949 Mobile Chamber of Commerce memo, four area foundries manufactured ornamental ironwork, mostly of modern floral design, which Mobilians enthusiastically embraced for their residences and businesses.[29] Though more modestly scaled than the nineteenth-century originals, this lacy iron imparted a romantic coastal feel to even the most generic modern buildings.

The tug-of-war between progress and preservation became more pronounced during the 1960s. There were heartbreaking demolitions as massive urban renewal projects resculpted the inner city. In the winter of 1962, dozens of historic buildings in a six-block area were torn down to accommodate a new municipal auditorium. Among the losses was a two-story 1840s brick structure affectionately known as the Old Spanish House, so called because it sat on an early Spanish land grant. Optimistic as ever, the *Mobile Register* reported that the bricks and iron balcony were to be salvaged, "so that the memory of the house will live on."[30]

Downtown Dauphin Street at dusk, looking east from the 600 block. In addition to original and reproduction ornamental balconies, this revitalized entertainment corridor also includes iron lampposts and trash receptacles.

The 1960s was a depressing decade for historic preservation in Mobile. Architects and planners, utilizing millions of federal dollars, intensified their efforts along the waterfront and downtown. Virtually all of the old warehouses on Front, Commerce, and Water streets—where forward-thinking merchants had so long ago petitioned for balconies—were leveled, as well as many fine antebellum town homes with elegant verandahs. Already reeling, preservationists were further staggered in 1965 by the demolition of the LeVert House, Marian Acker Macpherson's old home. One fourteen-year-old wrote the paper, "It's horrible. Can't somebody do something?"[31] The answer, unfortunately, was no. By decade's end, urban renewal had devastated Alabama's first city. More than two-thirds of the buildings carefully documented by the Historic American Buildings Survey were gone, the highest attrition rate of any American city. Entire neighborhoods had been obliterated, replaced by interstate highways, bleak public housing, and weedy empty lots.[32]

Amid the destruction, a formidable champion of Mobile's ironwork emerged. Margaret Rose Ingate loved her city and through diligent research learned a great deal about its cast iron traditions. Her work was professional, eschewing silly romance and rhetorical flights for hard facts. She tirelessly shared her knowledge through slide shows around the region and two feature articles in *Antiques* magazine. One of these pieces, "Mobile Ironwork," published in September 1967, presented the most cogent, comprehensive overview of the subject since Olive Brooks's 1929 essay. The article was so popular that the Historic Mobile Preservation Society sold offprints in its gift shop for years.[33]

Ingate worked hard to save as much ironwork as possible from the insatiable wrecking crews. In the fall of 1964, she wrote to a city official and requested permission to round up broken fences in the cemeteries. "Even though these pieces are beyond restoration in the fences," she explained, "they can be preserved as examples of the particular pattern."[34] When the historic Customs House (built 1852–56) was razed that same year, she managed to claim its massive gates for the city museum. Though she would have preferred for the ironwork to remain in its original location, Ingate had to be a realist. Today the Museum of Mobile holds an impressive collection of ironwork that, without her intervention, would otherwise have been scrapped.[35]

Opposite page: A restored section of the cathedral fence is guided into place, 2004. Originally erected in 1860 at a cost of five thousand dollars, its recent refurbishment was considerably more expensive.

Mobile's embattled preservationists finally got some much-needed help in 1973, when Margot Gayle, chairman of the Friends of Cast Iron Architecture, threw her support toward the effort to save the iron-fronted Elgin Building, threatened by urban renewal. In a letter to the editor of the *Mobile Register*, Gayle emphasized the building's importance as a "fine example of a type of 19th century American Architecture which is becoming more and more rare as the older sections of our cities are rebuilt."[36] With Gayle's help and lots of hard work by local preservationists like Nancy Holmes, director of the Mobile Historic Development Commission, a much-needed victory was finally achieved. The Elgin Building was placed on the National Register of Historic Places that March and the following year sold for commercial rehabilitation. Today the handsomely restored building continues to serve as professional offices.

Urban development did extensive damage to downtown's historic fabric. But by the 1980s enough old buildings remained to interest a new breed of developer more interested in saving historic architecture than knocking it down. Utilizing historic preservation tax credits, Jim Mattei and Allen Cox, a pair of local businessmen, restored Government Street's La Clede Hotel to its full grandeur in 1983. As far as these men were concerned, the hotel's spectacular balconies were a major attraction. "The first question is, 'Who has the right to the balconies during Mardi Gras?'" Cox joked with a *Mobile Register* reporter covering the project.[37]

Ila Cummings, right, and Cecilia Marie Woodford celebrate the restoration of the iron deer, Washington Square, September 2004.

Ever since the La Clede's successful restoration, balconies have once again proliferated downtown. Numerous building owners along Dauphin Street have added them (copying nineteenth-century patterns) and in some cases have applied for historic preservation grants to do so. Elizabeth Sanders, director of Main Street Mobile, a city agency devoted to downtown revitalization, recalled in an interview that one of Main Street's first grant requests was for a new balcony. Before it could be funded, however, one other preservation organization first had to get used to the idea. The Mobile Historic Development Commission's architectural review board (ARB), which approves all exterior work in the historic districts, initially balked at the request. In response, Sanders and her team put together a package that included old photographs of downtown balconies and convinced the ARB to approve the project. According to Sanders, balconies are a sound investment. "It's really about making second floor space attractive from a commercial or residential perspective," she said. She also recognizes Mobile's ironwork as character defining: "It is literally the thing that sets this town apart from the East Coast." Sanders engaged in other ironwork projects to enhance downtown. These included the 1994 restoration of the Bienville Square fountain and benches, as well as the installation of new iron trash receptacles and streetlights along Dauphin Street.[38]

In an effort to facilitate future downtown redevelopment of the type Sanders championed, the MHDC in 2000 formally updated its official policy on balconies. Its revised design guidelines read: "Original balconies or galleries should be preserved. Should documentation exist that a balcony or gallery was originally part of a building façade, the appropriate type of balcony or gallery may be added. Should there be no documentation that a balcony or gallery existed, a balcony or gallery appropriate to the age and character of the building may be added." Just as their nineteenth-century counterparts did, modern Mobilians enjoy balconies for protection from sun and rain or as a pleasant roost to sip drinks and watch the world go by.[39]

Burke Building. During the 1930s this building (pictured on page x as President Wilson would have seen it) lost its third story as well as its wrap-around two-story gallery. In 1988 a pair of attorneys restored the building and added a new gallery every bit as florid as the original. Downtown was back.

Other preservation organizations also turned their efforts toward cast iron restoration. The Friends of Magnolia Cemetery, founded in 1984, spent years carefully cleaning and restoring all of the cemetery's surviving ironwork, including the badly deteriorated Slatter Mausoleum. Troubling instances of theft were addressed by better security measures. The Church Street Graveyard Preservation Foundation cleaned and painted the ironwork in that cemetery in 1994. Ten years later, the Oakleigh Garden District Society fully restored the ever-popular iron deer to its antebellum luster, sans antlers, which were deemed too dangerous for clambering children.[40]

At the dawn of a new millennium, Mobile's ironwork still makes a strong impression, just as it did on Woodrow Wilson almost a century ago. In 2003 a transplanted schoolteacher named Diane Garden penned a short poem about her adopted home. "I can't believe we've moved to this city built on a swamp," she wrote. "The buildings are dripping lace like Spanish moss from the oak trees."[41] As Garden's lines demonstrate, after all the painful destruction and yearning for a modern metropolis, Alabama's port city remains firmly framed in iron.

Abbreviations

BA	Barton Academy
HMPS	Historic Mobile Preservation Society
MA	Municipal Archives, City of Mobile
MHDC	Mobile Historic Development Commission
MPL	Mobile Public Library, Local History and Genealogy Division
PC	Probate Court, Mobile County
USAA	University of South Alabama Archives

Notes

Preface
Ancient Echoes (Woodrow Wilson)

1. For a full account of President Wilson's visit, see *Mobile Register*, October 27–28, 1913.

2. Ibid.

3. The meeting bulletin's cover, reprinted in Harvey, "'Without Conscious Hypocrisy,'" 24, touts Mobile as "Queen City of the Gulf."

4. *Mobile Register*, October 27, 1913, 2–3.

5. For an excellent study of the diplomatic and economic ramifications of Wilson's Mobile speech, as well its local context, see Harvey, "'Without Conscious Hypocrisy,'" 24–45.

6. On Taylor's personality, see Thomason, *Mobile*, 161– 62.

7. Taylor, "Voice from Alabama," 55, USAA.

8. Ibid.

9. *Mobile Register*, October 27–28, 1913, describes the parade route and the crowds in detail.

10. Many of the buildings the president saw still stand, including Government Street Presbyterian Church, Barton Academy, and the Admiral Semmes House. For descriptions and/or photographs of the others, now sadly lost, see Gould, *From Fort to Port*, 208 (McGill Institute), 234–35 (Fidelia Club), and 161–62 (Alva Smith Vanderbilt Belmont House, known as the Murray F. Smith House).

11. Taylor, "Voice from Alabama," 56.

Introduction
Ornamental Cast Iron in American Architecture

1. On early America, see Gayle, *Cast Iron Architecture in America*, 34. On early Charleston wrought iron, see Poston, *Buildings of Charleston*, 31.

2. On Jay's Richardson House, see Mitchell, *Classic Savannah*, 38, 44. On Strickland's Second Bank, see Maynard, *Architecture in the United States*, 226; on his U.S. Naval Asylum, see Gayle, *Cast Iron Architecture in America*, 35, quote from p. 37.

3. Benjamin, *Builder's Guide*, 47.

4. Photographs and descriptions of the plantation houses appear in Lane, *Architecture of the Old South*, 65 (D'Evereux), 70 (Melrose), and 94 (Knox House).

5. For Wood's biography, see Lichten, "Philadelphia's Ornamental Cast Iron," 112. A description of the catalog appears in Nash, "'Lacy Iron,'" 236. A handful of Wood catalogs survives. The only one in the Southeast is at the Gallier House Museum in New Orleans.

6. *Godey's Lady's Book*, July 1853, 5–12, 7, 8, 9, and 12.

7. For rival foundries, see Nash, "'Lacy Iron,'" 238.

8. On the Perot partnership, see Nash, "'Lacy Iron,'" 257. The firm's many names by date are Robert Wood (1839–49), Robert Wood Iron Railing Foundry and Manufacturing (1849–57), Wood and Perot (1858–65), and Robert Wood and Co. (1865–81). On Wood's success see Howell e-mail, January 2,

2004. On the difficulties of design attribution, see Southworth, *Ornamental Ironwork*, 46–49. On Monroe's tomb, see Mitchell, *Hollywood Cemetery*, 3–4. On the number of Wood's employees, see Lichten, "Philadelphia's Ornamental Cast Iron," 113, and on business difficulties, ibid., 115.

9. For an excellent discussion of the conflicting definitions of these terms, see Maynard, *Architecture in the United States*, 174–76.

10. Sloan, *Model Architect*, 70.

11. Stevens, *Fashion and Famine*, 110.

12. Scully interview, June 8, 2004.

13. On the Verandah Hotel, see Scully, *James Dakin, Architect*, 53. On the 1855 fire, see ibid., 55.

14. *New Orleans Daily Picayune*, July 7, 1852.

15. King, *Great South*, 28.

16. Cable, *Old Creole Days*, 1–2.

17. Quoted in Lee, "Cast Iron in American Architecture," 97, 103.

18. Quoted in Nash, "'Lacy Iron,'" 231.

19. Downing, "Review," 229–30.

20. Masson, *Cast Iron and the Crescent City*, 4.

21. For a description of the *Hunley*, see Bak, *C.S.S. Hunley*, 49–50.

22. The Fiske visit and catalogs are described in "Ornamental Iron and Zinc Work," *Manufacturer and Builder*, 160–61, quote from p. 161.

23. Rydell, "Pearl Harbor," 1. On the ban of scrap iron sales to Japan see U.S. Dept. of State, *Peace and War*, 578.

24. Southworth, *Ornamental Ironwork*, 91.

25. On Gayle and the Friends of Cast Iron, see Lee, "Cast Iron in American Architecture," 112. On other preservation efforts, see Sledge, "Old Mobile Ironwork," 30.

Chapter One
Flowering: Mobile Iron to 1861

1. Waselkov, *Old Mobile Archaeology*, 20–21. The excavations were carried out by the University of South Alabama.

2. For descriptions of French Mobile (1711–63), see Thomason, *Mobile*, 34. An illustration of a typical French house with a wooden fence appears on p. 39. The physical characteristics of British Mobile (1763–80) are detailed on p. 43. A fascinating block-by-block tour of Spanish Mobile (1780–1813) is provided in Hamilton, *Colonial Mobile*, 501–9. Throughout the colonial period, travelers described Mobile as a small and unimpressive military outpost with a polyglot population.

3. Armes, *Story of Coal and Iron*, 14–15. For an appreciation of the importance of river and railroad work, see various foundry ads in the *City of Mobile Directories*, 1837–90.

4. *Mobile Daily Register*, October 26, 1833.

5. Biographical information on Spear comes from his obituary in the *Mobile Daily Register*, June 2, 1885, and Alderson from his obituary, ibid., March 24, 1859. The contract for the foundry is in Misc. Book C, 176–77, PC.

6. On the firm's services, see *City of Mobile Directories*, 1837–59. For the employees and their tasks, see *City of Mobile Directory*, 1859.

7. On Skates and Gazzam, as well as business revenue, see Amos, *Cotton City*, 212. For employees, see *City of Mobile Directory*, 1861. One of the machinists was William A. Alexander, who later worked on the Confederate submarine *Hunley*.

8. On Lang, see Ingate, "Mobile Ironwork," 3.

9. Amos, *Cotton City*, 212.

10. Parker, *His Promised Land*, 64–70; quotes are from pp. 64, 65, and 70.

11. Saxe-Weimar Eisenach, *Travels*, 40. This source also includes a description of the warehouse.

12. The Goodwin and Haire map is reproduced in Gould, *From Fort to Port*, 30. Because the scale is small, the original map should be consulted at the MA.

13. *Collection of the Ordinances, 1835*, 54. There are few extant iron balconies from the 1830s in Mobile. A disastrous 1839 fire downtown as well as urban renewal demolitions during the 1960s destroyed most commercial buildings from that decade. Additionally, older balconies were removed or replaced over the years.

14. The Collins and Barney contract is in Misc. Book C, 473–76; quotes are from pp. 473–74. The jail contract is in Misc. Book C, 379–87; quotes are from p. 386.

15. On the origins of Mobile's lamps, see Craighead, *From Mobile's Past*, 81–85 and the *Mobile Register*, January 26, 1947. On "lighting by the moon" see "Interesting Transcriptions from the City Documents," 1871–78, 298, MA. Carbon lights replaced gas lamps around 1900, and electric lighting was the rule by 1915. On more lighting in Bienville Square, see the *Mobile Daily Register*, September 21, 1859. On the number of lamps in 1864, see "Interesting Transcriptions from the City Documents," 1859–69, 88. On vandals see ibid., 1843–47, 3; and on damages by carriages, ibid., 1845–67, 98. Original lamps remain in front of Christ Episcopal Church and the Cluis-Rubira House at 156 St. Anthony Street. During the 1960s numerous salvage historic iron lamps were placed throughout the downtown, where they remain.

16. County Board of Education, Minutes, Vol. 1: 1836–45, p. 9. The winning bid is detailed on p. 25.

17. On Barton Academy, see Gould, *From Fort to Port*, 64–66.

18. Records of the Mayor, Envelope 3, Series 1, Box 8:3, MA. For the occupations of the signatories, see *City of Mobile Directory*, 1844, 1850. There is no directory for the year 1848.

19. Minutes of the Common Council, November 17, 1848, p. 392, MA.

20. *Code of Ordinances*, 1859, p. 183. There are no extant copies of the code between 1835 and 1859 so it is not known in exactly which year the new rules concerning verandahs took effect.

21. Amos, *Cotton City*, 193.

22. Gould, *From Fort to Port*, 129. For cotton exports and population figures, see McLaurin, *Mobile*, 42.

23. *Mobile Daily Advertiser*, February 4, 1854. On Alderson's agency with Gallagher, see *Mobile Daily Advertiser*, May 30, 1854, and on James and Chase, Brother, see *City of Mobile Directory*, 1859. On Ellison, see *City of Mobile Directory*, 1850, 1855 and *Eighth Census*, Mobile Co., Ala., 378, MPL.

24. *Mobile Daily Register*, September 28, 1852.

25. Ibid., December 13, 1852.

26. A description of the Battle House is in Gould, *From Fort to Port*, 148–49. It is not known whether Rogers's plans originally provided for a balcony. More likely, the local owners, being familiar with New Orleans and the Verandah Hotel, added it.

27. *Mobile Daily Advertiser*, January 2, 1855.

28. *Mobile Daily Register*, March 26, 1859.

29. On Bienville Square improvements, see Amos, *Cotton City*, 165.

30. See Diard Ironwork Ledgers, vol. 1, p. 414, HMPS. Ellison's successor, Daniel Geary, asked Wood if the pieces were ever paid for. There is no record of a response. See also Craighead, *From Mobile's Past*, 130. Craighead's account is filled with errors, but he interviewed Geary, who recalled the statues being placed "in order to stimulate the sale of some of the artistic productions of the Philadelphia house." To my knowledge, there are no extant photographs of the deer and Sambo together in the square. There is one poor quality image showing the deer on its mound, taken after a rare snowstorm.

31. On the deer in Victorian art, see Lichten, *Decorative Art*, 27–28.

32. On Wood and Sambo, Howell e-mail, January 2, 2004. Sambo does not appear in Wood's 1858 catalog, but the piece was available in the antebellum period. It does appear in post–Civil War catalogs. On Sambo in American art, Savage e-mail, August 24, 2004.

33. *Mobile Daily Register*, August 11, 1852.

34. "Interesting Transcriptions from the City Documents," 1815–59 (part 2), 343, 307.

35. *Illustrations of Iron Architecture*, 6. On the Elgin Building, see Gould, *From Fort to Port*, 163–64.

36. On Ellison's last order, see Howell e-mail, April 16, 2004.

Chapter Two
Postwar Trade: Brokers, Mongers, Builders

1. Delaney, *Confederate Mobile*, 23. A facsimile contemporary press account is reproduced but without a date.

2. *Mobile Daily Register*, October 24, 1863.

3. On Hutchisson, see Gould, *From Builders to Architects*, 45–47, quote from p. 45.

4. On the Geary household, *Eighth Census*, Mobile Co., Ala., 649.

5. Geary Papers, Roll 1, Trueheart Letter, January 1, 1863; ibid., Roll 3, Letter of January 13, 1863.

6. Geary Papers, Roll 2, Daily Dairy, April 11, 1865. On Geary disabling the guns, Bergeron, *Confederate Mobile*, 190.

7. *Mobile Daily News*, July 6, 1865.

8. Ibid., July 13, 1865. For years it was believed that Union troops threw Sambo into the river. One version of this legend is reported in the *Mobile Register*, June 7, 1936.

9. On the assets, see Administrative Account Book 23, p. 627. On debt, ibid., Book 71, pp. 550–51, PC.

10. Diard Ironwork Ledgers, vol. 1, p. 1, HMPS.

11. Ibid., pp. 7, 52.

12. Ibid., pp. 34, 44, 35, and 44.

13. There are numerous references to prices in the correspondence. For examples, see Diard Ironwork Ledgers, vol. 1, pp. 250, 265.

14. An order for stonework and encaustic tile is in Diard Ironwork Ledgers, vol. 1, p. 24.

15. On shipping problems, see Diard Ironwork Ledgers, vol. 1, pp. 119, 124.

16. Diard Ironwork Ledgers, vol. 1, loose letter dated April 17, 1867; ibid., p. 403.

17. *City of Mobile Directory*, 1869.

18. On Hutchisson's 1866 commissions, see Gould, *From Builders to Architects*, 47–48.

19. Diard Ironwork Ledgers, vol. 1, pp. 88–89, HMPS.

20. Ibid., p. 89.

21. Ibid., pp. 124, 91, 120, and 182. The 1860 census indicates that Patrick Kelley, a thirty-year-old carpenter, lived in the Rouse household. This may have been who Geary was referring to.

22. Diard Ironwork Ledgers, vol. 1, p. 180.

23. Ibid., p. 73.

24. Ibid., p. 190.

25. "Interesting Transcriptions from the City Documents," 1859–69, p. 239.

26. Diard Ironwork Ledgers, vol. 1, p. 190.

27. Ibid., p. 162.

28. The Pettus order, ibid., p. 86 and other orders, Howell e-mail, April 16, 2004.

29. Diard Ironwork Ledgers, vol. 1, p. 414.

30. Craighead, *From Mobile's Past*, 124.

31. Diard Ironwork Ledgers, vol. 2, pp. 287, 267, and 337.

32. King, *Great South*, 322.

33. Diard Ironwork Ledgers, vol. 2, p. 174; vol. 1, p. 165; and vol. 1, pp. 215–16. The resolution is detailed in vol. 1, p. 223.

34. Diard Ironwork Ledgers, vol. 1, p. 132.

35. Ibid., pp. 149, 161, and 165. For the verandah specifications, see ibid., p. 140.

36. Diard Ironwork Ledgers, vol. 1, pp. 235, 333, 338, and 344.

37. *Mobile Daily Register*, May 3, 1892. Geary is buried in Old Catholic Cemetery. On his estate, see Administrative Account Book 112, p. 345–47.

38. On Mobile foundries in the 1880s, see Berkstresser, "Mobile, Al. in the 1880s," 237. See also *City of Mobile Directory*, 1880.

39. Land, *Mobile: Her Trade*, 57.

40. American Historical Society, *History of Alabama*, vol. 2, 701. On Kling's association with Lang, *City of Mobile Directory*, 1869.

41. On marriage and family, American Historical Society, *History of Alabama*, vol. 2, 701.

42. *Mobile Daily Register*, August 31, 1884. On Hutchisson's design, see Gould, *From Builders to Architects*, 69. For years the Home Industry Foundry building was mistakenly associated with the construction of the *Hunley*.

43. *Mobile Daily Register*, November 13, 1884; November 8, 1884; and November 13, 1884.

44. Commercial Club, *Mobile Up to Date*, 71. This work also discusses Kling's commissions.

45. *Mobile Register*, November 18, 1918.

46. Mary Francis Alexander interview, November 3, 2003.

47. "Interesting Transcriptions from the City Documents," 1873–89, p. 75, MA.

48. *Mobile Daily Register*, March 31, 1890, and April 11, 1890. On the sale of the old Bienville Square fence, see "Interesting Transcriptions from the City Documents," 1820–1911, p. 383.

Chapter Three
Legacy: Romance, Ruin, Renaissance

1. *Mobile Daily Register*, April 9, 1892. There could well be earlier references to Mobile's ironwork by outsiders, but none has yet surfaced.

2. Fonde, "Mobile's Iron Lace," 7–8.

3. Carmer, *Stars Fell on Alabama*, 233.

4. *WPA Guide*, 204.

5. Fonde, "Mobile's Iron Lace," 7.

6. Brooks, "Old Cast-Iron," *New York Times*, September 8, 1929.

7. *Mobile Register*, 1932. No specific date, clipping in Ironwork vertical file, HMPS.

8. Goldfarb, "Etched in Time," 8.

9. National League of Pen Women, *Historic Homes*, 174.

10. *Birmingham News-Age Herald*, September 16, 1934. On HABS ironwork survey, see Gamble, *Alabama Catalog*, 178–79.

11. Frances Beverley, "Iron Lace," unpublished manuscript, 1935, p. 1. Ironwork vertical file, MPL.

12. *Mobile Register*, 1935. No specific date, clipping in Ironwork vertical file, HMPS.

13. Sledge interview, January 14, 2000.

14. *Mobile Register*, September 27, 1940.

15. Ibid., June 25, 1942. Ironwork vertical file, HMPS.

16. Ibid., n.d.

17. Quoted in Walker, *Literary Mobile*, 36. On World War II Mobile, see Thomason, *Mobile*, 209–46.

18. E. B. Sledge to Mary Frank Sledge, October 20, 1944, letter in author's collection. Sledge is the author of the famous memoir *With the Old Breed at Peleliu and Okinawa*. The incident referred to in the letter is not included in the book.

19. *Mobile Register*, January 14, 21 (sidewalks), February 19 (new sod), and January 9, 1947 (new benches).

20. Johnstone, "Iron as Ornament," June 1944 clipping with no attribution. Ironwork vertical file, MPL.

21. McNeely, *Bits of Charm*, xix.

22. Delaney, *Remember Mobile*, 152.

23. Howard, *Enchantment in Iron*, 6.

24. Walter, *Untidy Pilgrim*, 19.

25. *Mobile Register*, February 15, 1948.

26. Inge interview, July 7, 2004.

27. Inge, "Mobile Ironwork in Baldwin County," 2, MHDC. Hurricane Katrina seriously damaged this fence in August 2005.

28. "Iron Lace" brochure. Ironwork vertical file, HMPS.

29. Mobile Chamber of Commerce memo. Ironwork vertical file, HMPS.

30. *Mobile Register*, January 21, 1962.

31. Sledge, "Seeking a Future," 19.

32. On urban renewal, see Thomason, *Mobile*, 295. On HABS attrition, see Gamble, *Alabama Catalog*, 177.

33. On Ingate's lectures, see *Mobile Register*, January 21, 1966. See also Ingate's *Antiques* articles "History in Towns" and "Mobile Ironwork."

34. Ingate to Matthews, letter in Ironwork vertical file, HMPS.

35. On the Custom House demolition, see *Mobile Register*, April 11, 1965.

36. Gayle, letter to the editor, December 6, 1974, MHDC vertical file, 2 Water Street. This file also contains information on efforts to save the Elgin Building.

37. *Mobile Register*, February 27, 1983.

38. Sanders interview, April 28, 2004.

39. Lower Dauphin Street Commercial District Design Guidelines, MHDC.

40. On ironwork restoration in the cemeteries, see Sledge, *Cities*, 22 (Church St.) and 63–64 (Magnolia).

41. Walker, *Literary Mobile*, 232.

Glossary

acanthus. A neoclassical motif based on the leaf of a common Mediterranean plant.

alloy. A mix of two or more metals.

anthemion. A classical detail based on the palm leaf.

arabesque. An elaborate decorative pattern featuring naturalistic or geometric motifs. Common on porch or balcony railings.

cantilevered balcony. A balcony supported on brackets attached to the facade rather than from posts meeting the ground.

cast iron. Iron that is poured into a mold.

compression. To press together. Cast iron is strong in compression, hence its widespread use in columns.

cresting. An ornamental finish along a roof ridge or at the top of a wall.

crocket. Gothic motif representing stylized foliage commonly used to crown buttresses and gables. Frequently employed on iron fence posts during the nineteenth century.

drop frieze. A narrow ornamental band that is run just below an eave line.

gallery. A porch or balcony. From the French, *galerie*.

gazebo. An open-sided garden house.

Gothic Revival. A popular style during the middle to late nineteenth century. In ironwork it is manifested in fence patterns featuring lancet arches, trefoils, quatrefoils, and posts stylized as crockets.

Greek Revival. *See* neoclassical.

Italianate. Architectural style that flourished 1850–80. Influenced by the buildings and decorative arts of the Italian Renaissance. Ironwork includes florid verandahs on residential buildings and cast iron facades on businesses.

lancet. Narrow, pointed arch employed in Gothic architecture. Frequently used in fence patterns during the nineteenth century.

lunette. A semicircular opening over a window or below an arch.

neoclassical. Style popular throughout the nineteenth century, influenced by ancient Greek and Roman architecture and decorative arts. In ironwork it is manifested in numerous motifs, including Greek key designs, lyres, anthemion cresting, and acanthus leaves.

piazza. Porch.

picturesque/rustic. Mid-nineteenth-century decorative arts philosophy that celebrated naturalistic and romantic themes. Elaborate floral iron fences and railings are common examples of this sensibility.

portico. A formal porch attached to a building, usually supported by columns.

quatrefoil. Four-lobed, clover-shaped Gothic motif common in cemetery ironwork. Symbolizes the four Gospels.

rinceau. An ornamental band, usually featuring vines or some repetitive pattern, frequently employed along fence bottoms and on drop friezes.

tensile. Of or relating to being pulled or stretched. Cast iron has poor tensile strength.

trefoil. A trilobed Gothic motif commonly used in cast iron cemetery fences. Symbolizes the Trinity.

verandah. A covered porch or balcony.

wrought iron. Iron that has been worked by a blacksmith with hammer and tong. Often used in fences in conjunction with cast iron finials.

Bibliography

Archival Sources

Administrative Account Books. PC.

City of Mobile Directories, 1837–1901. MA.

Code of Ordinances of the City of Mobile. Mobile: Goetzel & Co., 1859. MA.

A Collection of the Ordinances Now in Force in the City of Mobile, 1835. Mobile: *Mercantile Advertiser*. MA.

County Board of Education. Minutes. Vol. 1: 1836–45. BA.

Diard Ironwork Ledgers, 2 vols. HMPS.

Geary Papers, 3 rolls. MPL.

Inge, Mary Jane. "Mobile Ironwork in Baldwin County." Unpublished manuscript, n.d. MHDC.

"Interesting Transcriptions from the City Documents of the City of Mobile." Vols. for 1815–59 (part 2), 1820–1911, 1843–47, 1845–67, 1859–69, 1871–78, 1873–89. Prepared from original data by the Municipal and Court Records Project of the Works Progress Administration, 1939. MA.

Ironwork vertical file. HMPS.

Ironwork vertical file. MPL.

"Lower Dauphin Street Commercial District Design Guidelines," revised June 29, 2000. MHDC.

Minutes of the Common Council. Council Minutes, roll 16. MA.

Miscellaneous Books. PC.

Records of the Mayor, Board of Aldermen, and Common Council. General Files, 1848. MA.

Sledge, E. B. to Mary Frank Sledge, October 20, 1944. Letter, author's collection.

Taylor, Richard Vipon. "A Voice from Alabama." N.d. USAA.

U.S. Bureau of the Census. *Eighth Census of the United States, 1860. Population*. Mobile County, Ala. MPL.

Vertical files. Various properties. MHDC.

Interviews and Personal Communications

Alexander, Mary Francis. Interview by author, Mobile, Ala., November 3, 2003.

Howell, Ann. E-mails to author, Mobile, Ala., January 2; April 16, 2004. MHDC.

Inge, Mary Jane. Interview by author, Mobile, Ala., July 27, 2004.

Sanders, Elizabeth. Interview by author, Mobile, Ala., April 28, 2004.

Savage, Kirk. E-mail to author, Mobile, Ala., August 24, 2004. MHDC.

Scully, Arthur. Interview by author, Mobile, Ala., June 8, 2004.

Sledge, E. B. Interview by author, Montevallo, Ala., January 14, 2000.

Newspapers

Birmingham News-Age Herald, 1934.

Mobile Daily Advertiser, 1854–55.

Mobile Daily News, 1865.
Mobile Daily Register, 1833–92.
Mobile Register, 1904–2004.
New Orleans Daily Picayune, 1852.

Books, Articles, and Other Sources

American Historical Society. *History of Alabama and Her People*. Vol. 2. Chicago: American Historical Society, 1927.

Amos, Harriet. *Cotton City: Urban Development in Antebellum Mobile*. Tuscaloosa: University of Alabama Press, 1985.

Armes, Ethel. *The Story of Coal and Iron in Alabama*. Boston: Cambridge University Press, 1910.

Bak, Richard. *The C.S.S. Hunley: The Greatest Undersea Adventure of the Civil War*. Dallas: Taylor Publishing Co., 1998.

Benjamin, Asher. *The Builder's Guide*. Boston: Perkins and Marvin, 1839.

Bergeron, Arthur, Jr. *Confederate Mobile*. Jackson: University Press of Mississippi, 1991.

Berkstresser, Alma Esther. "Mobile, Al. in the 1880s." Thesis, University of Alabama, 1951.

Brooks, Olive. "Old Cast-Iron Work in Favor." *New York Times Magazine*, September 29, 1929.

Cable, George Washington. *Old Creole Days*. New York: Scribner's, 1879.

Carmer, Carl. *Stars Fell on Alabama*. New York: Farrar and Rhinehart, 1934.

Commercial Club. *Mobile Up to Date: Its Port and Industries Graphically Portrayed*. Mobile: Mobile Stationery Co., 1895.

Craighead, Erwin. *From Mobile's Past: Sketches of Memorable People and Events*. Mobile: Mobile Printing Co., 1925.

Delaney, Caldwell. *Confederate Mobile: A Pictorial History*. Mobile: The Haunted Book Shop, 1971.

——. *Remember Mobile*. Mobile: Gill Printing Company, 1948.

Downing, Andrew Jackson. "Review: Greenwood Illustrated." *Horticulturist* 1, no. 5 (Nov. 1846): 229–30.

Fonde, Elizabeth. "Mobile's Iron Lace." *American Riviera Review*, August 1929, 7–8.

Gamble, Robert. *The Alabama Catalog: A Guide to the Early Architecture of the State*. Tuscaloosa: University of Alabama Press, 1987.

Gayle, Margot, and Carol Gayle. *Cast Iron Architecture in America: The Significance of James Bogardus*. New York: Norton, 1998.

Goldfarb, Stephen J. "Etched in Time: The Art of Marian Acker Macpherson." *Alabama Heritage* 73 (Summer 2004): 6–13.

Gould, Elizabeth B. *From Builders to Architects: The Hobart-Hutchisson Six*. Montgomery: Black Belt Press, 1997.

——. *From Fort to Port: An Architectural History of Mobile, Alabama, 1711–1918*. Tuscaloosa: University of Alabama Press, 1988.

Hamilton, Peter J. *Colonial Mobile*. Boston: Houghton, 1910.

Harvey, Gordon E. "'Without Conscious Hypocrisy': Woodrow Wilson's Mobile Address of 1913." *Gulf Coast Historical Review* 10, no. 2 (Spring 1995): 24–43.

Hinckley, C. T. "A Day at the Ornamental Ironworks of Robert Wood." *Godey's Lady's Book,* July 1853, 5–12.

Howard, Anne Shillito, with illustrations by William D. Howard. *Enchantment in Iron*. Mobile: Rapier House Publications, 1950.

Illustrations of Iron Architecture, Made by the Architectural Iron Works of the City of New York. New York: Baker and Godwin, 1865.

Ingate, Margaret Rose. "History in Towns: Mobile, Alabama." *Antiques* 85 (March 1964): 294–309.

——. "Mobile Ironwork." *Antiques* 92 (September 1967): 354–59.

King, Edward. *The Great South*. Hartford, Conn.: American Publishing Co., 1875.

Land, John E. *Mobile: Her Trade, Commerce and Industries 1883–84*. Mobile: Mobile Printing Co., 1884.

Lane, Mills. *Architecture of the Old South: Mississippi and Alabama*. Savannah: Beehive Press, 1997.

Lee, Antoinette J. "Cast Iron in American Architecture: A Synoptic View." In *The Technology of Historic American Buildings: Studies of the Materials, Craft Processes, and the Mechanization of Building Construction*, edited by H. Ward Jandl. Washington, D.C.: Foundation for Preservation Technology, 1983.

Lichten, Frances. *Decorative Art of Victoria's Era*. New York: Scribner's, 1950.

——. "Philadelphia's Ornamental Cast Iron." *Antiques* 62 (August 1952): 112–15.

McLaurin, Melton and Michael Thomason. *Mobile: The Life and Times of a Great Southern City*. Woodland Hills, Calif.: Windsor Publications, 1981.

McNeely, S. Blake. *Bits of Charm in Old Mobile*. Mobile: Gill Printing Company, 1946.

Masson, Ann M. *Cast Iron and the Crescent City*. New Orleans: Gallier House, 1975.

Maynard, W. Barksdale. *Architecture in the United States, 1800–1850*. New Haven: Yale University Press, 2002.

Mitchell, Mary H. *Hollywood Cemetery: The History of a Southern Shrine*. Richmond: Virginia State Library, 1985.

Mitchell, William Robert, Jr. *Classic Savannah: History, Homes and Gardens*. Savannah: Martin-St. Martin Publishing Co., 1991.

Nash, Julia. "'Lacy Iron': Nineteenth-Century American Ornamental Castings and Robert Wood of Philadelphia." *Pennsylvania History* 34, no. 3 (July 1967): 229–39.

National League of Pen Women. *Historic Homes of Alabama and Their Traditions*. Birmingham: Birmingham Publishing Company, 1935.

"Ornamental Iron and Zinc Work." *Manufacturer and Builder* 10, no. 1 (Jan. 1878): 160–61.

Parker, John P. *His Promised Land: The Autobiography of John P. Parker, Former Slave and Conductor on the Underground Railroad*. New York: W. W. Norton, 1996.

Poston, Jonathan H. *The Buildings of Charleston: A Guide to the City's Architecture*. Columbia: University of South Carolina Press, 1997.

Rydell, Roy. "Pearl Harbor and Hawaii's Labor History." *People's Weekly World*, June 21, 2004, 1–3.

Saxe-Weimar Eisenach, Duke of (Bernard). *Travels through North America during the Years 1825 and 1826*. Vol. 2. Philadelphia: Carey, Lea & Carey, 1828.

Scully, Arthur. *James Dakin, Architect*. Baton Rouge: Louisiana State University Press, 1973.

Sledge, John. *Cities of Silence: A Guide to Mobile's Historic Cemeteries*. Tuscaloosa: University of Alabama Press, 2002.

——. "Old Mobile Ironwork." *Alabama Heritage* 24 (Spring 1992): 22–31.

——. "Seeking a Future for the Past: Historic Preservation in Mobile." *Mobile Bay Monthly,* May 1992, 18–20.

Sloan, Samuel. *The Model Architect*. Philadelphia: E. S. Jones, 1852.

Southworth, Michael and Susan. *Ornamental Ironwork*. Boston: David Godine, 1978.

Stevens, Ann S. *Fashion and Famine*. New York: Bunce and Brother, 1854.

Thomason, Michael V. R., ed. *Mobile: The New History of Alabama's First City*. Tuscaloosa: University of Alabama Press, 2001.

U.S. Department of State. *Peace and War: United States Foreign Policy, 1931–41*. Publication 1983. Washington, D.C.: U.S. Government Printing Office, 1943.

Walker, Sue, John Hafner, and Mary Riser, eds. *Literary Mobile*. Mobile: Negative Capability Press, 2003.

Walter, Eugene. *The Untidy Pilgrim*. New York: Lippincott, 1953.

Waselkov, Gregory. *Old Mobile Archaeology*. Mobile: University of South Alabama, Center for Archaeological Studies, 1999.

The WPA Guide to 1930s Alabama. 1941. Reprint, with an introduction by Harvey H. Jackson III. Tuscaloosa: University of Alabama Press, 2000.

Index

Note: Italicized page numbers refer to photographs and their accompanying captions.